DAD'S WISDOM

A Blueprint for Life

by
Alex Alvarez

Dad's Wisdom: A Blueprint for Life. Copyright 2023 by Alex A. Alvarez. All rights reserved. No part of this book may be used or reproduced without prior written permission from the author, except in the case of brief quotations embodied in critical articles or reviews, provided that the name of the book and the author are clearly cited. Chapter dividers by pikisuperstar/Freepik. Cover image by epicstockmedia/123RF.

ISBN 978-064-688850-7

BISAC Heading Suggestions:
FAMILY & RELATIONSHIPS / Parenting / Fatherhood
SELF-HELP / Motivational & Inspirational
SELF-HELP / Personal Growth / General

1.0

A. A. Alvarez Publishing
aaalvarezpublishing@outlook.com

This one is for you, Alexandra.
You made everything better.

Table of Contents

Find Your Why: Mine Was You 7

Practice Resilience and Gratitude: Keep Your Chin Up 11

Develop Your EQ: Know Others, Know Yourself 19

Make Lifelong Friends: Lead, Laugh, Connect, Contribute 29

Manage Chaos: Become a Pillar of Strength 37

Keep Yourself Together: Respect Your Body, Own Your Space 47

Cultivate a Growth Mindset: Turn Learning Into a Hobby 59

Nurture Your Ambition: Strive for Greatness 69

Learn Finance: Master Cash Flow and Compounding 81

Invest Well: Choose Your Partner Wisely 91

Find Your Family: Bond with Purpose 105

Plan Beyond: Nurture Your Nest 111

Embrace Your Mortality: Live Well, Leave a Legacy 119

Recommended Reading 127

About the Author 135

"The mystery of human existence lies not in just staying alive, but in finding something to live for."
Fyodor Dostoevsky

Find Your Why: Mine Was You

My dear Alexandra,

Before you ever took your first breath, before I ever held your tiny hand in mine, I loved you. I knew you. In my heart, I felt you, a whisper of a dream that turned into my most cherished reality. Your existence, even as a mere thought, shaped my life in ways I could never have imagined.

I often sat and wondered who you would be, what you would look like, and how your laughter would sound. Would you have your mother's eyes, perhaps my nose? Would you pick up her ability to stay out of trouble or my tendency to find it? What myriad of attributes will become uniquely yours?

Knowing that you would one day come into our world fuelled my every decision, my every step. You've always been my guiding star, a beacon illuminating my path even long before you were born. Every major decision I have ever made has been driven by a duty to become a better man, to support your mother, to provide our family with the freedom and the privilege of choice, and to leave a lasting legacy. But above all, it's been for you.

When I learned that we were going to have you, I knew it was right. A profound connection, an unbreakable bond had already formed, and having you made me infinitely happy and fulfilled. It also terrified me. I brought you into this world, and from that point forward, I knew you'd forever become the centre of my universe. I thought you already were, but boy, was I wrong. Expecting you was one thing. Having you in my hands was another thing entirely, and it was the single most significant moment of my life.

When I said I brought you into this world, I didn't mean it figuratively. I meant it literally. I never left your mother's side, and I jumped at the opportunity to welcome you into our family. I was the one who held you for the first time, the one who severed your last physical bond with your mother, and the one who laid you on her warm chest. When you joined us in our hectic alien world, you were first a little dazzled by the bright lights, but you remained calm and curious. You stared intensely at me, as if you already knew who I was, and felt safe in my hands. And I mean that figuratively, because literally, you were slipping fast and I had to recruit a third hand to prop you up.

I am painfully aware that there will come a time when I can't hold you again, when I can't comfort you with my own voice. But my words, our memories, and the lessons I'll share here shall forever be with you. Know that you gave my life purpose, and because of you, I lived it to the fullest.

Our story as a family is one of triumphs and struggle, of learning and growth, of privilege and gratitude. And though you're still a blissfully sheltered little girl, your spark, your curiosity, your empathy and your love compel me one last time to document my thoughts, my experiences, and my reflections, so that I can continue guiding you as you grow up to become the author of your own destiny.

Although you still love colouring rainbows, you already show wisdom beyond your years. So, think back to this age and remember to treat your life as you treated each canvas as a child, because you still have the power to paint it with the most vibrant colours. Embrace the love, the laughter, and even the pain, for it is all part of the majestic artwork that is your existence.

You are my baby, my greatest joy, my proudest achievement. And though words could never fully capture the depth of my feelings for you, I wrote this book to help you discover what you're made of, to remind you of who you are, and to demonstrate what you've always meant to me.

I also hope that this humble compilation of experiences and wisdom helps you form your own blueprint for life, but please promise me that you'll take what you read here with a grain of salt. This week you said something new, something beautiful. You said that you love me just the way I am, and then gave me a hug and a tender kiss. But I'm still a flawed man and my views are biased, so think critically about what I'm saying. Does it apply to you, is it valid or are these just the ramblings of an old man stuck in his ways?

That's up to you to decide, but whichever the case may be, know that these pages are a place where you can find me; a place where you can hear my voice and feel cuddled once again. I will always be with you. Here, in your memory, and in your heart . . . as you will forever be in mine.

I love you.

"If you're going through hell, keep going."
Winston Churchill

Practice Resilience and Gratitude: Keep Your Chin Up

When I embarked on my lifelong journey as an expatriate, I was driven by a dream; not about a better life for myself, but a better life for the children I imagined having. You know the story of how I met your mother in my early teens and how I instantly knew I would marry her one day. But what you may not know is that even before I met her, I already knew your name. That's how present you've always been in my life, and how long I had to travel to finally reach you.

As a young man full of hopes and dreams, working towards building that better life, I faced adversity head-on, often enduring soul-crushing sacrifices. But I never let up. I studied new languages, learned to cope with prejudice and rejection, and became a chameleon able to gracefully adapt to strange environments and cultures. It was a hard road, but in time, I got to recognise that the very challenges I was facing were instead privileges; experiential gifts that helped me develop the resilience I needed to become a good father.

As I matured, I learned to turn my trials and tribulations into something positive, not just for me, but for you, and for everyone who supported or inspired me along the way. These gifts came with that responsibility and became not just the weight that kept me grounded, but also the wings that allowed me to soar.

There's a saying dating back to the French Revolution that you most likely learned from a Spiderman movie. It is that with great power comes great responsibility. Privilege is much the same, except it's not nearly as obvious. We don't always notice when we have it, but we surely feel its absence when we don't. From my humble beginnings to the awards and successes I sporadically enjoyed throughout my life, I've had the privilege of shaping my future, and that's something I've never taken lightly. Your grandparents' struggles, the safety they provided me, the countless doors opened by my many mentors, my able body and my sharp mind, even being born in my third-world country—all of these were privileges. We must recognise our advantages and use them to help others. I want you to explore my journey, my struggles and sacrifices, but also the joy of my achievements. These experiences are not just mine; they are ours, shaping me, shaping your mother, shaping you.

My path towards becoming a citizen of the world was littered with strong emotions. Some of the most prevalent were the loneliness of leaving behind the familiar, the excitement of broadening my horizons, the torment of rejection, and the bliss of acceptance. But as I moved from one country to another and bonded with other cultures, I learned that what we share as humans is far greater than what we don't. Our family's multicultural heritage, our challenges and adventures, our stories of pain and joy—these are not merely anecdotes. They are the experiences that taught me the lessons that shaped my world view.

Our society may be filled with dichotomies, but it's also filled with beauty and understanding. So, welcome the differences, find common ground, and try to see the world through a lens of compassion and empathy. You don't have to travel much to begin to understand humanity, but I recommend that you do. Immerse yourself in other cultures with an open mind and an open heart, and dare to witness the richness of diversity, my dear. It's a treasure trove of wisdom, spice, and incalculable value.

Embrace Your Privilege and Be Grateful
The concept of privilege can sometimes be challenging to understand, as it's often misconstrued. Nevertheless, it's a reality for all of us, albeit to varying degrees, and that's perfectly okay. In life, we don't always get to choose the cards we're dealt. So, when you find yourself holding a good hand, don't feel guilty about it; just be grateful. Seize every opportunity to succeed, because you'll inevitably get some bad hands as well, and you'll need to learn how to play those with equal determination.

I want you to understand, sweetheart, that the importance of recognising and embracing your privileges lies in turning them into something positive. This isn't a lesson learned overnight, and many people struggle to grasp it. But for you, my love, I want you to see that privilege can be a catalyst for growth, for empathy, and for making the world a better place. Never deny it, and never apologise for it. Just use it for good.

The tears of joy I shed when Australia welcomed us with open arms weren't just about relocating to a place that recognised our worth. They represented the realisation of a once-distant dream and a testament to the hard work that led us here. It served as a lesson in gratitude, a reminder to appreciate every success, because life's outcomes, whether good or bad, often involve an element of luck and the involvement of others. It's crucial to never overlook the beauty and fragility of the world around you, and to be grateful for the good fortune in your life. Luck plays a significant role in the equation of success, so always hold gratitude in your heart and take a moment to cherish everyday victories. The pain of a loss far outweighs the joy of a win, so relish your victories whenever they come, for it often takes many to offset a single loss.

Gratitude is more than a fleeting sentiment; it's a way of living. It's the art of cherishing a stunning sunrise, a kind gesture, a completed project, and a loving family. It's enjoying a concert, a New Year's fireworks display, or a nice meal at a restaurant with your phone in your pocket. This embodies empathy, appreciation for the present moment, and inner contentment.

In our journey through life, with its blend of struggles and triumphs, we find ourselves woven into the fabric of existence and influenced by the threads of chance. How we celebrate our accomplishments, how we uplift others, how we live each day; all this is what defines our character, and it's how we'll be remembered after we're gone. So, if you ever wonder what the point of living is, know that this is it.

Adapt or Pivot
You may have learned that when I was your age—and I mean your age now that I'm writing this, not when you're reading it—I was what some called an "old soul". Family and even strangers would jokingly predict that at the rate I was going, I would grow up to become either the next Simón Bolívar—the revolutionary oligarch who led the liberation of Venezuela, Colombia, Peru, Bolivia and Ecuador from Spanish rule in the 1800s—or the next Adolf Hitler.

I, on the other hand, already had the feeling that technology, not autocrats, would eventually rule us all. So, I leaned towards becoming an electrical engineer. At the time, computers weren't yet a common household appliance. And come to think of it, by the time you read this, they'll probably have been replaced by something else entirely.

Life, however, had other plans for me. There were missteps, setbacks, and plenty of what some might label as failures. But were they legitimate failures or were they instead opportunities to learn valuable lessons and pursue more fitting goals? For instance, sacrificing in Greece what could have been my most productive years, after relinquishing my chance to establish roots in the United States, left me feeling like I had let down those who had once believed in me. I grappled with a sense of personal failure, a feeling that I might never recover. Growing up, especially after having been dubbed "Most Likely to Succeed" in high school, I believed I was destined for greater things. Now, instead, I feared being locked in an endless game of catch-up, doomed to spend the rest of my days not building a better future, but reminiscing about the man I could have been.

I realise this may sound harsh, perhaps even melodramatic, but make no mistake: in my mind, it was a personal hell. Those years represented the lowest point in my life. Not necessarily because they were objectively difficult, but because my mind was consumed with thoughts of how I had squandered my potential by placing myself in an environment where someone with my personal and physical attributes seemed destined to remain perpetually stuck at the back of a queue that led nowhere. And even though my interpretation of the situation had merit, my fixation on it magnified my suffering far beyond what was necessary for me to grow from it.

Now that I know better, my dear, I want you to know that finding obstacles along life's path isn't always a bad thing. As the saying goes, necessity is the mother of invention. It can serve as the spark that kindles your inner strength. A meaningful struggle can empower you to explore uncharted territory, to unlock new opportunities, and to discover treasure where others can only see dirt. Most importantly, it can reveal your true character, for it's through adversity that both you and the world get to understand what it is you're made of.

My pilgrimage through Greece taught me much. It taught me about the value of friendship and community, about the dangers of lowering my standards to suit temporary conditions, and about recognising sunk costs and learning to let go. It inspired me and your mother, even when we thought we could least afford it, to travel throughout Europe while we were still young enough to enjoy it but with the maturity we needed to behave responsibly. And it also forced us to develop the shared vision that led us to Australia, and eventually, to you.

Our bad times compelled us to grow up together as a single unit, and the hard lessons we learned enabled us to quickly surpass our expectations later in life when we finally started playing at a table where the deck wasn't so stacked against us. But the key takeaway from all this is that if we had not gone through that period of despair, we would have never made Australia our home, and you, our greatest joy, would never have completed our family.

Every deviation from my original path led me to something more profound: my relationship with your mother, my dynamic career, our precious family, a life well lived. What appeared as failures at the time turned out to be doorways to something more meaningful and satisfying. The immediate outcomes weren't always positive, but in hindsight, I learned to accept that the pain I endured often served as a catalyst for my personal growth, both as an individual and as a citizen of the world. I discovered purpose not by following a predetermined roadmap but by remaining adaptable, by embracing failure as a learning opportunity, and by uncovering possibilities in the unexpected.

So, don't let the fear of change paralyse you, my dear. Your journey may twist and turn, but remember, it's all part of the adventure. You'll eventually discover that sometimes, the sweetest and most profound victories are achieved by approaching your goals from different angles, not necessarily by pursuing them head-on.

But let's not romanticise it either. The path to establishing a stable and prosperous world for you was much harder than it needed to be for us to feel a true sense of accomplishment. Nevertheless, through unwavering determination, a hint of stoicism, and a lot of resilience, we eventually reached our destination. This is why, if there's one key takeaway from this assortment of seemingly disparate reflections, it is that with love, discipline, diligence, and focus, even in the face of failure, you too can succeed.

> *"Knowing others is wisdom.
> Knowing yourself is enlightenment."*
> Lao Tzu

Develop Your EQ: Know Others, Know Yourself

I grew up in a world obsessed with Intelligence Quotient (IQ) as a measure of a person's ability to contribute to society. But my life experience, especially my journey as a migrant, taught me that it is those with strong emotional intelligence, or as it is measured, Emotional Quotient (EQ), that are most likely to succeed and make the world a better place. As it turns out, life has a peculiar way of leading us down winding paths, introducing us to people of all backgrounds, and presenting us with opportunities to grow. So, I want to share with you some lessons I've learned along the way to help you navigate the world with a deeper understanding of not just others, but also yourself.

Empathy for Survival
Empathy helps us bridge the gap between what's familiar and what's foreign. It is the ability to put yourself in someone else's shoes, to feel what they feel, and to understand their point of view even when you don't share it. It's a skill that allows us to connect with people on a profound level, transcending language, cultural and even ideological barriers.

The vivid memories of my childhood that I carry to this day are mostly characterised by a theme of empathy in one way or another. At your age, I could not understand why adults did not care to make any effort to try and see the world from my perspective. It wasn't until I grew a little older that I began to realise that I also was not too concerned about trying to see the world from theirs. These were the initial sparks of my awakening as a human being capable of understanding others. But it was in my early teens that I started to realise that developing my emotional intelligence wasn't just good for my wellbeing, but critical to my survival. You see, Venezuela was neither a safe nor a kind place, especially to young males like me who made a habit of standing up for themselves and for others less capable. Any slip-up, faux pas or failure to accurately read a social situation could quickly escalate to someone getting seriously hurt or even killed. So, I learned to hold my tongue in tense situations—though your mother might disagree. I also learned to proactively deescalate conflict and to quickly and honestly apologise when I found myself out of line. Hopefully you won't have to learn the hard way like I did.

Venture Outside Your Comfort Zone
Purposely developing my emotional intelligence early in life not only kept me alive and out of serious trouble, but it was tremendously helpful after I left Venezuela and faced a far less hostile society in the United States. It was still a daunting experience—a new country, a new language, and a sea of unfamiliar faces. But in those moments of alienation, I found solace in my ability to connect with others.

Imagine being in a land where you don't speak the language, where you don't understand the culture, and where every social interaction feels like a puzzle where you hold the four corner pieces but don't quite know how far apart to place them. It's in those moments that you realise how vital it is to listen, to observe, and, most importantly, to empathise with others. I discovered that a warm smile or a simple gesture of kindness could transcend language and convey emotions that words alone couldn't express.

As you now know, my journey didn't end in the United States. My journey eventually led me to the pebbled beaches of Greece, and lastly to the sandy shores of Australia. With each move, I encountered new cultures, traditions, and perspectives. And one thing I learned is that the world is a catalogue of experiences; some that you don't get to choose, some that you never discover, and some that are ripe for the taking. Each one represents a unique story, a different way of looking at life. It's easy to remain confined within the boundaries of our own borders and social circles, but true growth occurs when we step outside our comfort zone and embrace diversity.

Living among people from various backgrounds, I discovered that our differences are not to be feared but celebrated. Diversity enriches our lives, broadens our horizons, and teaches us the beauty of tolerance and acceptance. It is through understanding and appreciating these differences that we can most effectively develop our emotional intelligence.

Here's what's most remarkable, my dear. As I strived to understand those around me, I found that I was also getting to know myself better. When you open your heart and mind to others' experiences, it's like holding a mirror to your own soul. You start to recognise your own biases, your greatest strengths, and your most embarrassing weaknesses too.

By learning to see the humanity in others, I gained insight into my own. I began to understand the roots of my emotions, the reasons behind my actions, and the impact I had on those around me. It was a journey of self-discovery that continues to this day. So, remember this as you go through life: Developing your emotional intelligence is not just about understanding others; it's a path to enlightenment, a way to know yourself deeply. It's about empathy, embracing diversity, and using these insights to become a better, more compassionate human being. And don't forget to use that compassion to be kind to yourself too.

Cultivating Emotional Intelligence
Emotional intelligence is not a feeling or a state of mind. It's a skill that must be developed, trained and nurtured like any other. Here are some practical tips to help you develop your EQ.

1. Listen Actively
One of the cornerstones of emotional intelligence is active listening. It's not solely about hearing the words; it's about trying to understand the emotions and intentions behind them. So, when you engage in a conversation, try to be fully present. Put away distractions, maintain eye contact, and show interest in what the other person is saying. By doing this, you not only build stronger connections with others but also gain valuable insights into the way they experience the world and how they feel about it.

2. Practice Self-Control
Understanding yourself is equally essential to developing your EQ. Take time to reflect on your own emotions and reactions. When you feel a surge of anger, sadness, or joy, pause for a moment and ask yourself if an outburst is appropriate (hint: sometimes it is). The ability to pause and think before reacting is

the key to managing your emotions and becoming an effective leader. And when you've got the time to ponder about your emotions, keeping a journal or simply writing about your experiences can become a powerful habit for self-reflection. Documenting your thoughts and feelings can help you uncover patterns and behaviours that you can use to your advantage. For example, when you're feeling at your worst, reading an old journal entry about when you thought all was lost—when it wasn't—can help keep you grounded by reminding you that this too shall pass.

3. Keep at It
Empathy isn't a one-time event; it's a lifelong practice. Make it a habit to put yourself in other people's shoes. Especially in difficult situations, ask yourself how they might be feeling or why they might perceive a situation a certain way. By continually honing your empathetic skills, you'll not only deepen your connections with people but also gain a broader perspective on life.

4. Be Mindful and Meditate
I am mindful, but I don't meditate like most other self-professed mindful people do. The mere thought of sitting with my eyes closed and focusing on my breathing stresses me out. I'm just not that kind of person. Instead, I write, walk, play a videogame or hit the gym. The point of meditation is to clear your head and help you calm down, and in my case, these other activities do precisely that. Whichever way you lean, practices like these can help you relax, allowing you to observe your emotions without judgment, training the awareness muscles that will improve your ability to respond to stressful situations with more clarity and self-control. So, my advice is to just do whatever works for you.

5. Choose Your Tribe Wisely

Your support group, your circle of trust, your tribe — whatever you choose to call it — is essential. These are the individuals who've earned your trust, those with whom you can lower your guard and be vulnerable. Choose them carefully, consult with them, and consider their input. It takes courage to ask for constructive feedback, but it's a valuable way to enhance your emotional strength. Others may notice aspects of your behaviour that you might overlook, providing opportunities for growth. However, exercise caution when seeking advice, as not everyone in your tribe, especially outside of it, is qualified to offer the guidance you might be after.

6. Beware of Free Advice

Please baby, don't ever listen to or take advice about any topic from anyone who has not clearly achieved more than you have on that given domain. Don't take love advice from those whose relationships have failed. Don't take business advice from those whose ventures aren't thriving. And never ever take financial advice from those who have less than you.

People from all walks of life are eager to give advice, but most of it is rubbish. Even if you recognise it as such and have the wisdom to never follow it, merely listening to it can still negatively affect your heart and mind. Except for your mentors, those who have achieved success and have worthwhile advice to give, don't waste their time giving it away. They charge handsomely for it. Moreover, the most expensive advice is often free advice. Remember this, for it can influence every aspect of your life, for better or for worse.

7. Have the Courage to Be Disliked

Not everyone will like you. That's a fact. The sooner you make peace with that, the happier you'll be and the more you'll appreciate the friends you make. Having the courage to be disliked gives you a sense of freedom that few things can match. It helps you break free from the social shackles that limit our potential.

As humans, we are wired to seek approval from others; it's a survival instinct that dates back to our tribal days. Back then, being liked meant that you were welcome in the tribe, that you'd survive the winter, whereas being disliked meant that you'd get banished and would likely starve or freeze to death. But life is better now and the stakes are not as high.

You might be wondering, "Why risk being disliked at all?" The thing is, when you have the audacity to stand your ground, you create room for your authentic self to shine. It allows you to be genuine, to speak your mind, and to act according to your values—not society's expectations. Plus, being disliked by some is often a sign that you're doing something right. It means you stand for specific values or beliefs, and as a result, you'll attract people who genuinely value the real you.

In the modern world, the concept of likeability is often manipulated. Social media platforms have turned approval into a currency, but at what cost? We see influencers and even our own friends bending over backwards to be palatable to the masses, sacrificing their own individuality. And even though the risk of being disliked can serve as a check and balance in a civilised society, when you're not constantly bogged down by the weight of everyone's expectations, you become lighter and nimbler in your journey through life. This empowers you to no longer survive like most people and allows you to thrive instead, without needing to develop sociopathic tendencies in the process. You'll also become more emotionally resilient, and believe it or not, people will admire you for it because everyone knows that it takes immense courage to be unapologetically you. The payoff is immense.

So, seize the courage to be disliked and be your own person. You're not here to win a popularity contest; you're here to live a fulfilling life, on your own terms. And remember, being disliked by some doesn't make you unlikable; it makes you an individual who's capable of independent thought.

Strengthening Emotional Resilience
As you develop your emotional intelligence, you'll inevitably discover emotional resilience. A higher EQ equips you with the tools to navigate life's challenges with grace and composure. It doesn't mean that you won't face difficult moments or that you won't break at times; it means that you'll be better prepared to handle yourself when that happens.

With strong guidance from my older siblings throughout my formative years, I've worked hard on developing my EQ my whole life. This lifelong commitment has allowed me to bounce back from all kinds of setbacks with newfound strength. As a youngster, I faced the very real risk of dying in an act of violence. After I left home, I faced the very real risk of being sent back. Since my early twenties, no matter how fit or otherwise healthy I've been, I've faced the very real risk of having a heart attack. In my thirties, I faced the very real risk of staying crippled after a freak sports accident. And last year, soon after I hit forty, I got cancer and it's been a brutal battle since. Such is life, my dear. It's full of sadness and despair, but also full of joy and opportunity. That's what makes it beautiful.

Have there been times when I thought all was lost? You bet. Have there been times when I just broke down in solitude and felt like banging my head against the wall? You bet. But have I picked myself up anyway and done what needed to be done, if not for me, for your mother, and lately, for you? You bet.

Emotional resilience is not about suppressing your emotions. It's about channelling them productively so you can carry your burdens gracefully and still fulfill your purpose. So, don't think for a second that resilience is all about ignoring your suffering. Rather, it's about persevering in spite of it.

The pursuit of self-improvement and self-determination is a lifelong commitment, and nurturing your EQ enriches your understanding of others as well as your understanding of yourself. As you embark on your own journey, remember that empathy is not just a skill; it's a profound way of connecting with the world that will not only enrich the lives of those around you but also your own.

"True friendship multiplies the good in life and divides its evils."
Baltasar Gracián

Make Lifelong Friends: Lead, Laugh, Connect, Contribute

The most significant gifts you can give to yourself and others are the gifts of love, friendship and understanding. Think about your closest friends. What makes those connections special? It's often the feeling that you can confide in one another, share your joys and sorrows, and know that you'll be met with empathy and support, without harsh judgement. These are the kinds of friendships that enrich your life, and they do so in immeasurable ways.

Everything good that has ever come my way, everything I've ever achieved, and every moment of joy in my life can be directly linked to my connection to others. None of it would have been possible on my own. Even when these special people are not active participants in my triumphs, simply being there to witness the feat and be genuinely happy for me was often helpful enough.

While you should be intentional in forging connections with people, this practice should never be transactional because, as we just explored, empathy forms the foundation of meaningful and long-lasting relationships.

When you aim to understand and begin to internalise what others are going through, you build trust and emotional bonds that stand the test of time. Empathy also plays a vital role in creating a sense of belonging. When you extend compassion and understanding to others, you make them feel valued and accepted. In turn, you create an environment where people feel safe to be themselves around you, and they will, in turn, extend the same freedom to you.

It is also wise to make a habit out of performing regular acts of kindness. Simply giving someone the opportunity to talk about their day or offering a comforting word when they're down on their luck can have a profound impact on their life.

Sometimes, the most powerful display of love is to be present for someone, to offer a shoulder to lean on, and to remind them that they are not alone. Your mere presence can be a beacon of hope for someone in need in their darkest hour or even their brightest moment, for people can also find themselves alone in the best of times. Think about how being that person would make you feel. Think about how that could enrich the life of those around you, and especially, your own.

I suppose a lot of this might seem obvious to you. If you're still the kind, funny and clever Alexandra that I know today, I trust you'll already have a wonderful circle of friends with whom you've connected well, with whom you can laugh loudly, and with whom you share a strong bond centred around the contributions you make to each other's lives and the world at large. For a highly energetic extrovert like you, finding people you like will be the easy part. But these traits also expose you to expanding your circle far more than you should, and because of that, I'd like to give you some fatherly advice about how to approach disputes and about the importance of culling the herd.

Navigating Conflict

By now, you'll have undoubtedly learned that life is not without turmoil. Disagreements and misunderstandings between people are bound to happen, but with the right level of emotional intelligence, and a fair understanding of negotiation techniques—which you'll hone down when you go to business school—you can glide through most of these with grace.

My mother taught me never to fight with my mates unless I was ready to call it quits for good. To hammer her point home, she warned that if she ever caught me squabbling with a friend, she would personally make sure we'd never hang out again. She wasn't trying to scare me off disagreements altogether, but to make me think twice before escalating any argument. So whenever I found myself in a heated moment, I would pause and ask myself, "Is this a good enough reason to end this friendship?"

I've parted ways with many people, but never in a fit of anger or impulsiveness, and I'm pleased to say that I've never had a messy breakup—not with a friend or even with the girlfriends I had in my early teens before your mother swooped in and permanently took me off the market.

So, when you find yourself in a conflict, pause to reflect on the bigger picture and give genuine thought to the other person's perspective. Try to understand their feelings and motivations. By doing so, you'll often find common ground and solutions that benefit you both. You've probably heard that the magic word is "please," but I've got something even more effective for you: a magic question for conflict resolution. That question is, "What would it take?"

This magic question was a gift from Zoe Chance, one of my lecturers in business school. By framing the issue this way, you can nudge the direction of most disputes towards an actual resolution, as it empowers the other party to change their emotional state from "defending" their point of view "against" yours to instead, "work with you" to reach an agreement, knowing that they've had their needs met.

Say you're leading a university project and one of your teammates admitted that they won't be able to turn in their work on time. You and your other teammates could either waste your energy arguing about how unfair this is, how you'll all now get poor marks because one person didn't deliver or you might even start turning on each other. Alternatively, if none of you is qualified or has the resources to pick up the slack, you could ask, "What would it take for you to turn in your work on time?" The answer might surprise you. Perhaps they are simply exhausted because renovations in their apartment building are not letting them sleep and their electricity keeps cutting out, limiting their ability to work on the project. All they might need is a place to stay for a few days, and the solution to that problem is easy. Someone in the team could host this person, allowing you all to get what you want, and if that person is you, now you get to make a new friend. How good is that?

This technique is useful in all negotiations, whether you're dealing with a co-worker, your broker, your spouse or even your child. But remember, it's not about winning arguments but about preserving harmony and finding a solution to a common problem. This is especially true when you're negotiating with your spouse. As the old saying goes, "You can choose to be right or you can choose to be married."

Too Much of a Good Thing
Throughout my life's journey, I've witnessed the profound impact of connecting with people of all kinds. When you empathise with others, you're more likely to engage in acts of kindness and compassion that have the power to heal wounds, bridge divides, and create a brighter future for you and those around you. But try to imagine a world where everyone practices unrestrained empathy. What would that look like? At first glance, it may seem like a utopia where everyone is seen, heard, and appreciated for who they are — a fully inclusive society. However, for such a world to exist, one must set one's values aside to forcefully empathise with absolutely everyone, regardless of how flawed or evil their agenda might seem. So, even though empathy is a remarkable quality, it is essential to balance it with another virtue: tolerance. Learn the difference.

Do not betray your core values, force yourself to like people that repulse you or make it your life's mission to find common ground with every ideologue you encounter. Be critical in your thinking and do your best to base your reasoning on logic, not emotion. I trust you'll recognise which forces are striving for the greater good and which forces only seek to destroy. And beware of movements, especially those championed by young people. Their hearts might be in the right place, but they still lack the maturity, the life experience and the historical context to understand the repercussions of having their demands met.

Be Selective
Good friends are easy to recognise. They are understanding, they are dependable, and they enjoy your happiness and feel

your sorrow as if it were their own. But as important as it is to recognise good people and welcoming them into your circle, it is perhaps more important to learn to recognise parasites so you can rid yourself of their influence. Beware of individuals who are either cynical, unambitious or conformist. They are dangerous company and will never tire of leading you astray by pulling you down to their level. They have the power to cloud your judgement and derail you from your righteous path by draining you of your positive energy and filling your mind with fear and doubt. When you strive to push forward, they'll encourage you to settle down. When you choose to face your demons, they'll advise you to yield. When you try to improve yourself, they'll assure you that you're good enough. They will sound like friends. They might even believe that they genuinely care about you. But they don't. They just want you to be like them because you are most definitely not like them. You are better. So, cut them loose and cut them early. I promise you that you won't miss them, and I guarantee you that they won't miss you. Your mere existence, to such people, is nothing but a reminder of their own failure to define a worthwhile purpose for the one life they were given — the one they chose to squander with their mediocrity. It's a pity and a shame for them to be this way, but it's not your cross to bear. It's theirs and they bought it. Let them carry it.

Later, when I recommend that you uplift others and welcome the chance to become someone's mentor, I won't be referring to leeches that suck you dry of your ambition. I'll mean those who do put in the effort. Those who have the aptitude and the attitude to do better in life, but who may lack the knowledge, the resources or the guidance to fulfil their potential.

To Each Their Own

Not every friend must fulfil every emotional need. That would only lead to perpetual disappointment and loneliness, so it's crucial to set realistic expectations. There is an unlimited number of roles into which you and your friends can fit to complement each other's lives, so choose what works rather than trying to be everything to everybody. There are gym friends, golf friends, dinner friends, school friends, work friends, business friends, and friends that help you lift heavy furniture. With some luck, a few of your friends may be able to serve multiple roles. However, attempting to discuss a business idea or sharing an emotional dilemma with a friend who doesn't align with that role could strain the relationship that made your friendship work in the first place.

Trusting or sharing a particular need with someone who does not fit that category is a violation of the very trust they had in you to know better. If you feel vulnerable, reach out to your emotional friend. Likewise, if you feel like hiking on a Sunday morning, don't ever call your party friend! Learn to understand these boundaries and don't jump in with both feet if you ever wish to cross them. Test the waters first. This has helped me make friends from all walks of life that I can count on (for the right need) and who can equally count on me.

Moreover, I strongly advise you to not strive to be anyone's "everything" friend. That's a tall order to fill and one that will inevitably lead to conflict and disappointment. Likewise, don't expect anyone to become your "everything" friend. No friend will ever be capable of satisfying all your needs, not even your husband. And that's a good thing. If you've paired up well, you'll see that he'll agree.

Real Friends Are Forever

True friends offer empathy, support, and a sense of belonging. They multiply the joys and divide the sorrows, enriching our existence in immeasurable ways. As you navigate through life, remember to cherish these connections, but also be discerning in choosing friends who uplift and inspire, for they can all play a unique and meaningful role in your life. Cultivate relationships that align with your values and aspirations, and don't be afraid to let go of those who drain your energy and rob you of hope. Friendship is a priceless gift; cherish and cultivate it wisely, for it will be a source of strength and joy throughout your entire life.

> *"Be the useful person at the funeral,
> the one on whose shoulders other people cry."*
> Jordan Peterson

Manage Chaos:
Become a Pillar of Strength

Life has a knack for throwing our plans off course. I once dreamed of becoming an electrical engineer, and for a fleeting moment, may have also considered leading a revolution or even conquering Europe. But as I grew older and began making my own mistakes, my dreams shifted. Ironically, what I perceived as failures often turned out to be lessons guiding me towards something more profound, something that mattered. Your journey too will have twists and turns with moments of doubt and perceived failures. But remember, my dear, that sometimes the most meaningful victories come in unexpected ways. Be open to change because uncertainty is ubiquitous and learn to find joy in the journey itself.

Imagine being in a typhoon, waves crashing around you, and strong winds tossing you in every which way. And yet, amid the chaos, there's an eye to the storm, a place where all is calm. My cancer journey, more than any previous experience, taught me to seek that eye, that centre, and to become a pillar of strength, not just for myself but also for those I love — especially you.

Life can be wicked. It throws curveballs when you least expect them. Just when I thought I had it all—a loving family, a valuable career, a strong body and good health—I heard the dreaded words, "You've got cancer." Having done my own research, I had been suspecting it for months, but I still held on to the foolish hope that I might have been wrong. Unfortunately, I wasn't, and as the doctor explained how bad the prognosis was, all I could think of was you. To think that there are parents whose children fall ill is beyond heartbreaking.

As everything I had been dreading suddenly became a reality, I felt disappointed, scared, and angry. But more than anything, I felt cheated. Yet, in that ugly mess of emotions, there was clarity—I had you, my reason for everything, my "why." And after I left the hospital, I couldn't help but think that if it had been you in my shoes, I would have done anything to trade places. Maybe that's what happened in an alternate universe, so perhaps we're the lucky ones.

Before all of this, I used to go on long walks at night, with headphones on, and there was a non-zero chance I'd get hit by a bus in one of those dark and quiet streets. So, what would I have done if that happened? It's likely that in that last second, right as the headlights came at me at full speed, I'd wish for a few more months so that I could give you and your mother a softer landing. Thinking that maybe I did get hit by a bus, and that these were the few extra months I wished for, kept me from wallowing in misery and gave me a renewed sense of purpose and resolve. Reframing reality in such ways helped me tremendously to cope with my sorrow so I could remain strong and useful.

I'm not saying this to appear brave. Quite the opposite. I'm saying it because I feel helpless knowing that the outcome of this is not up to me. It's just a matter of waiting, hoping that my remission lasts, and that I land on the right side of a seemingly arbitrary survival rate.

I had to endure watching you see me transform from a healthy and active dad—someone who lifted heavy weights, practiced martial arts, and chased you around the playground until "you" were the one who got tired—into a weak, hairless shadow of a man who couldn't even lift you. So, knowing what was coming, I took preemptive measures to reframe your perspective. I let you know that I'd be losing some hair, so I'd be shaving my head to not look like I had a fight with a cat. You laughed. I showed you photos of handsome bald men and assured you that I'd look just as cool. You even started looking forward to it. But I also told you that I was sick, and that I was going to remain sick for a while; that I'd be spending time in hospitals, and that the doctors would do everything in their power to make me better.

I didn't tell you I could die soon, but I did teach you that it was possible to die from illness—at the time, you believed that people would only die when they turned 100 years old. You then asked me, "Are you going to die?" and I answered that we're all going to die at some point, but nobody knows when. That's what makes life worth living, and that's why we do what we do. I asked you, "If you knew that you were going to die tomorrow, then what would be the point of brushing your teeth?" We had many such conversations, and because of that, you never felt stressed about my situation. Instead, you adapted. You learned to hug me gently while I recovered from each surgery. You were understanding when I couldn't play with you like I used to. You started washing your hands the instant you got home from school and learned to be watchful of what you touched outside so that you wouldn't bring germs home.

Talking to you this way and treating you like a rational human being instead of a mindless child, did not scare you. It empowered you. It helped you accept your new responsibilities. It showed you that I trusted you, and that you could trust me.

I didn't complain much either. How could I? Your mother had her hands full as your primary carer. She was also juggling housekeeping responsibilities and work pressures while keeping up with my frequent medical appointments. So, I sheltered her from having to witness my physical and emotional decline. She already had enough on her plate, like contemplating a future without her husband, and the prospect of having to shoulder by herself the immense load of responsibilities that I had amassed over the years, on top of her own. The last thing she needed was to see her husband defeated.

Therefore, when I didn't look fine, I acted fine. I even moved to the guest room so she wouldn't witness my terrible nights and fevers. And during the day, when I could not physically act fine, I would go for a "nap" and lock myself in my room where neither one of you could see me twisting in pain, contemplating the possibility that that day could be my last. I also built her a comprehensive handover plan in case I died suddenly, because between the disease and the treatment, my vital organs were brought to the brink of collapse. Yet, I did not abandon my responsibilities. I continued managing our finances, all while solving disputes and negotiating day in and day out with banks, brokers, lenders and insurance companies to preserve your patrimony. Now more than ever, I had to stay sharp and on top of everything. This was not the time to "take it easy and focus on my healing" as some suggested. What a man can do, a man must do, and the same principle applies to you.

Because I held my own, your mother held her own too, and you were not robbed of your future. Together, we managed to preserve everything we had built, and because of that, your happy childhood, to this day, remains uninterrupted.

I cannot bear the thought of how different things would have turned out if I hadn't been so intentional throughout my life in developing my resilience and increasing my emotional quotient so that one day, I'd be prepared for this moment, to handle this situation as if it were business as usual.

For a while, I even started to lose my mind—not in the sense of going crazy, but in the literal sense of the word. Chemotherapy was melting my brain cells too, so I felt as if I were developing Alzheimer's disease. This was terrifying, especially because I was fully cognisant of the abilities that I was losing each week. Names, dates, short and long-term memory, concentration, and focus. So, what did I do? I enrolled in a cybersecurity course, even though that's not my field. I studied hard, took an exam, and proceeded to earn the relevant industry certification. Like a muscle, the brain needs training. And like a muscle, the rule is "use it or lose it." After that, I enrolled in another course, and another, and another. In just a few months, I accumulated a wide range of qualifications that helped me achieve multiple objectives: they helped restore my cognitive abilities, they enhanced my professional skills, and as a nice bonus, they gave me a competitive edge when I defied my doctor's orders to not re-enter the job market before my new immune system was ready to be tested out in the real world.

I spent countless hours in the hospital, undergoing chemo, with a textbook in my hands and doing courses on my mobile device. Did I really need to do this? Yes. Why? Because I could. If I survived, it would make me a more effective professional, able to co-create more value. And if I didn't, I would rather die knowing that I kept pushing, especially when I had every excuse not to. More importantly, I wanted you to know that I chose to live my remaining time on this Earth moving forward, not giving up. I wanted you, and the world, to know that I'll always give 100% and that my family can rely on me, no matter what, not only while I'm here but also after I'm gone. This gives me a profound sense of satisfaction and inner peace. Therefore, being strong in the face of adversity is not crushing; it's liberating. It makes the unbearable bearable and allows you to thrive in the worst of circumstances.

Dealing with my diagnosis reconfirmed my belief that when the chips are down, it's your ability to manage chaos that sets you apart. The key to resilience is adaptability. Cancer forced me to adjust my sails, to pivot without losing sight of where I wanted to go. Your mum and I had to juggle doctor's appointments, balance work and home, and figure out how to cope and prepare for the worst—all while making sure that we still had some quality time as a family.

Just like the captain of a ship steering through a storm, I had to show up every day, come what may. But it wasn't just about being stoic. It was about becoming a pillar of strength for those who depended on me. You needed your dad to be a dad, even after a stage 4 diagnosis. But there's no greater motivator than seeing your innocent eyes and knowing that now, more than any other time, I must remain strong and continue striving for excellence, for you.

Becoming a pillar of strength doesn't mean you don't wobble. I wobbled, stumbled, and sometimes felt like I was about to collapse—both physically and emotionally. It's important to feel your emotions; it's human. There were days when all I wanted to do was lay in bed and escape. But escaping isn't managing chaos; it's avoiding it. So, even on the days I felt like crumbling, I rose because that's what pillars do—they rise and stand tall, and they carry the heaviest burden, not just for themselves but for the structure with which they've been entrusted.

Managing chaos involves recognising the uncertainties of life and navigating them with poise. It's about knowing that even in your darkest hour, there's light within you. And for me, that light was you.

So, how do you become this unwavering pillar? First, you've got to recognise when you're dealing with a wicked problem—an intricate challenge that's tough to tackle because it's riddled with inconsistencies, shifting variables, and elusive requirements that are often hard to pinpoint. Ignoring the chaos only leads to more confusion. Second, take stock of what you can control, like your attitude, your actions, and your words. And finally, remember your "why," your core reason that keeps you steadfast.

Managing chaos is as much about self-awareness as it is about action. It's understanding your limitations and strengths, and then playing your cards accordingly. During my treatment, there were days when my body was so drained that even standing felt like an uphill battle. But I also went hiking one day after I had chemotherapy just so I could say that I did. Still, I was aware of my limitations and knew that pushing myself too hard would only make things worse.

This is where the art of delegation comes into play. I had to swallow my pride and let others help me, whether it was letting your mum handle housekeeping or allowing friends to pitch in by bringing us meals, picking you up from school, or even with financial support.

The old me, the pre-cancer me, would have taken this as a blow to my ego. But the wiser, pillar-of-strength me understood that sometimes, leaning on others is the best way to stand tall. You cannot be a rock all the time. Like Bruce Lee once said, sometimes you must be like water, ever flowing and adapting.

You're probably too old now to remember this, but recently, there was a weekend when I felt particularly down, and you approached me with your coloured pencils and a piece of paper and asked me to draw with you. I wasn't in the mood and didn't have the energy either, but your innocent enthusiasm was too contagious to resist. We spent that afternoon drawing and creating a world of our own, a world far removed from hospital visits and financial stress. In that moment, you were my pillar of strength and taught me that pillars come in all sizes, even in the size of a cute little five-year-old.

Something else I learned from this ordeal is that you can't afford to ignore your mental and emotional well-being. I've had bouts of anxiety and despair that loomed like dark clouds, threatening to soak my spirits. To keep them at bay, I did not turn to meditation. Again, that's just not how I roll. Instead, I turned to action and continued fulfilling my role as the head of our household, with your mother as the body that supports me and with you as the heart that gives us both purpose. I also journaled—documenting my thoughts, my fears, and insights—and used those musings to put this book together for you. Writing is therapeutic, like talking to an old friend or mentor who offers you a listening ear and an open heart. It also helps you declutter your thoughts and organise your ideas. And for me, at least, achieving and maintaining order—within me and around me—clears my mind.

Here's another piece of advice. Take it from someone who has stood face-to-face with the grim reaper: Practice laughing at yourself and the absurdities of life; like when I told you that staying at the hospital was like staying in a hotel, but one where strangers turn the lights on and wake you up every half an hour to tell you off for not resting. Even at your young age, you got the irony of that scenario. In a sea of chaos, humour can be a lifesaver. It's not about making light of the situation; it's about shedding light on the darker corners of your ordeal.

Becoming a pillar of strength isn't just about you; it's about the profound impact you can have on others. When life gets hard, people need someone to look up to, a guide through the murkiness, a lighthouse peering through the fog. By managing chaos effectively and holding strong under pressure, you become that guiding light. You'll be surprised by how people rally around someone who stays composed when everyone else is losing their cool. This is not just a responsibility; it's a privilege. It gives your life an extra layer of meaning. The more you serve as that rock, the more you understand your role in the grander scheme of things. You will not just be surviving; you'll be helping others survive too, and nothing crystallises your purpose more than that.

You'll also find that being the one that others can lean on gives you unparalleled clarity in your own life. The issues that once seemed monumental suddenly become trivial when you're carrying more than just your own weight. You develop an acute sense of what really matters, allowing you to shed the pettiness that often occupies our minds. After being diagnosed, I no longer had time for frivolities. I had a daughter to protect, a legacy to build, and a life to rescue. Your life becomes a well-edited film, only containing scenes that truly matter. And let's not forget this basic, undeniable truth: it's the right thing to do.

Becoming a pillar of strength aligns with some of the deepest virtues that humanity cherishes—altruism, compassion, and integrity. When you make the conscious choice to be strong for others, you're not just contributing to their lives, but you're enriching your own. It's a virtuous cycle; the more you give, the more you get back. Love, respect, gratitude—they all flow back to you, tenfold.

So, my little one, as you grow into the person that I trust you'll be, aim to be that pillar of strength. It won't be easy; you'll have to face your own challenges, swim against fierce currents, and sometimes, you might find yourself standing alone. But the reward is an unshakeable core, a life lived with purpose and meaning—a legacy you can be proud of.

*"First say to yourself what you would be,
and then do what you have to do."*
Epictetus

Keep Yourself Together: Respect Your Body, Own Your Space

Self-respect begins the moment you wake up and gaze at your reflection in the bathroom mirror. Who do you see? A dishevelled mess rushing through the morning or someone who takes a moment to appreciate their worth? Every time you look into the mirror, you're not just staring at your physical attributes—you're glimpsing into a self-constructed reality. If you like what you see, you carry that positive energy into your day. If you don't, well, that's a different story altogether.

You Are What You Project
We're often told to not judge a book by its cover, but let's be real: the cover does tell you something, sometimes a lot. Not the full story, of course, but who would buy a book first, read it, and then decide if it's worth buying? It doesn't make sense. The cover gives us a glimpse into what the book is about, and that's often all it takes for us to either take it home or leave it on the shelf. With us humans, this process of judgement isn't much different; the way we carry ourselves—the respect we show for

our bodies and our environments—casts a clear reflection. It signals to the world who we are and what we stand for, but more importantly, it also shapes how we feel about ourselves.

When you walk into a room, your presence sends a message. If you're not put together well or your space is chaotic, it speaks volumes, and not in your favour. But when you keep yourself together—mentally, emotionally, and physically—you exude an aura that makes people take notice. That aura isn't just for them; it's for you. The more respect you have for yourself, the more respect you gain from others. This is not about putting on a façade. It's about making your ideal self your personal baseline, creating a virtuous circle that keeps elevating you throughout life's highs and that can sustain you throughout life's lows.

Fit as a Fiddle: A Lifetime Investment
The billionaire investor, Warren Buffett, wasn't mincing words when he said that if you could only ever own one car, "You're probably going to read the owner's manual four times before you drive it; you're going to keep it in the garage, protect it at all times, and change the oil twice as often as necessary. If there's the least little bit of rust, you're going to get that fixed immediately so it doesn't spread—because you know it has to last you as long as you live." This analogy is a stark reminder that we get just one body in this lifetime, so why wouldn't we treat it with the utmost care?

Spending time, money and effort in physical fitness is not a narcissistic endeavour. It is an investment that pays daily dividends and offers compounding returns. I'm not just talking about lifting weights or hopping on an elliptical machine three to five times a week. Living an active lifestyle can mean a lot of different things—walking regularly, swimming, cycling, or even playing beach ball with your mates. The key is to find an activity that you enjoy and turn it into a habit. You don't have to aim for Olympic gold to treat your body right. If you're fairly fit, a good diet and regular activity will do the trick. But if you're starting from behind, you'll need to put a lot of extra effort just to catch up.

Fortunately, exercise has a powerful flow-on effect. When you take care of your body, you become more resilient to stress, have higher energy levels, and your mental clarity sharpens. It's a feedback loop of wellbeing that influences every aspect of your life, from your work performance to your personal relationships.

I must admit, though, I haven't always been fit. But that's perfect because it helps me drive my point home. As I shared earlier, my time in Greece wasn't enjoyable, and that's putting it mildly. This negatively impacted my self-esteem, my overall outlook on life, and filled my mind and spirit with a crushing feeling of, "What's the point?" So, despite arriving in my early 20s as a slim athlete with a six-pack, as this feeling of hopelessness compounded, I didn't just stop caring; I stopped looking.

Around the time I hit thirty, I remember staring in the mirror in the morning, without a shirt on, and for the first time in a long time, I paid attention—and did not like what I saw. It was as if my veil had been lifted. My biggest shock was thinking, "How long have I looked like this and how could I not notice?" Immediately, I got to work. For as long as I remembered, I had been fit and slim, so I never felt the need to learn about exercise and nutrition. I thought that if I only started jogging for an hour a week and did a hundred push-ups a day, that I'd get back in shape in four to six weeks. How naïve of me! Confessing this level of ignorance today is embarrassing, but I'm doing it anyway because it's also hilarious.

When I jumped on the treadmill for the first time, I felt like a monkey astronaut, but without the training. "How do I operate this thing?" I asked myself. Once I finally got going, I was spent within seconds. Over time, however, I got better and began to pick up steam. I learned that what I needed to reclaim my body was muscle, so I switched my training approach and focused on that. But too often, I skipped days or was too lax at the gym. So, I hired a trainer for the days I had made a habit of skipping, because if there's anything I hated more than being weak and out of shape, it was to waste money. This was a fantastic investment, because not only did it keep me going, but it also taught me a lot about the law of diminishing returns.

In time, the gym became my sanctuary, a space where I'd not only improve my physique but also clear my mind, because physical fitness isn't just about what you see in the mirror; it's about how it makes you feel on the inside—stronger, more focused, and more capable.

Still, I scoff when I see personal trainers in their 20s lecturing men and women in their 40s and 50s about how getting fit and staying fit is all about going to the gym three times a week and maintaining a specific caloric balance. That's like being the child of a billionaire and lecturing desperate 20-year-olds on how easy it is to retire rich if only they could spend less than they earn. Being fit in your 20s is ridiculously effortless. All you need to do is nothing; nothing to sabotage yourself, that's it. But after a man's dwindling testosterone levels plummet with age or after a woman has had a child or two? Fat chance! Being fit after life has had ample time to play all its dirty tricks on you requires one of two things: superior genetics or a phenomenal amount of effort and dedication from the instant you wake up to the moment you close your eyes at night.

Newton's First Law—The Law of Inertia, states that an object at rest will stay at rest, and an object in motion will stay in motion, unless acted upon by an external force. In simpler terms, things tend to keep doing what they're already doing unless something else interferes. And when it comes to people, when given the choice to do nothing, a person's first instinctive response is to do nothing. Choosing otherwise requires clarity, willpower and strong mental conditioning. So, my dear, since you'll be reading this for the first time in your teens or in your early 20s, the best advice I could give you regarding fitness is to stay in shape, for this is far more achievable, and far more sustainable, than staying in shape after having to get fit in the first place.

Taking care of your physique isn't an isolated act; it impacts your entire being and the quality of your life. Do not see it as a chore, but as an act of respect to and a show of gratitude for the unique vessel that is your body.

The Clothes Maketh the Man
This adage has been around for centuries for good reason. Its literal interpretation can be misleading, but its essence remains universal—your appearance matters.

When you put on a nice outfit, look in the mirror, and are pleased with what you see, you'll carry that positivity with you. Dressing well isn't an exercise in vanity; it's a form of self-respect. It's not about impressing others; it's about impressing yourself and valuing who you are. When you feel good in your own skin, people around you sense it too. Your confidence blooms, influencing how you're perceived, which, in turn, affirms your self-worth. Dressing well then becomes a tool for empowerment.

Dismissing the impact your appearance has on how others perceive you—and more importantly, how you perceive yourself—would be foolish.

You wouldn't rock up to a first-date or an important job interview dressed in an outfit that screams, "I don't care," right? Why? Because deep down, you know that when you present well, you're effectively saying, "Hey, I'm worth the effort." Those initial judgements that people make about you based on your appearance aren't trivial—they can lead to gaining greater access to the best opportunities or to having doors slammed shut in your face. Take your pick. But always remember to dress for yourself first. Whatever opportunities or respect that flow from your appearance are merely bonuses.

A Place for Everything: Own Your Space
How you treat your environment—your home, your workspace, even your car—is a direct reflection of your inner state, of your mental and emotional health. Maintaining cleanliness and order is not about being obsessive or neurotic; it's about respecting yourself enough to maintain an environment that's conducive to productivity, inner peace, and clarity of mind.

The psychological impact of our surroundings is commonly underestimated. A messy room, even for those who claim that that's how they like it, feeds the muscles of procrastination and brings forth cycles of inefficiency and sloth. Alternatively, when everything's in its rightful place, your mind is free to focus on what really matters. In this clean and organised state, you're ready to welcome opportunities and relationships that enrich your life and, likewise, you will reject those that clutter it further.

But let's be real, keeping things neat and tidy isn't always easy. Life happens and chaos is sometimes inevitable, especially with free-spirited children around. When this happens, it's not about how pristine you can keep things, but how you adapt and restore balance. It's a sign of maturity, resilience, and self-regard. Remember, it's your space and you dictate its energy and vibe. You are a rare five-year-old child, and that's a good thing. You've become a product of your upbringing, so you are not a terribly messy child. Sure, when you play, you make a mess of things, but you recognise that they are a mess and when it's time to clean up, you understand what cleaning up means. You are used to living in a clean and tidy environment and seeing your mommy and daddy cleaning up after themselves, never leaving the house in disarray from one day to the next, no matter how tired they may be. To you, order is normal. Order is what's right. I have a feeling you'll grow up just fine.

Beyond aesthetics and productivity, a well-maintained space signals to others how you value yourself and, in turn, how they should value you. When you invite people into a clean, orderly space, it becomes a hospitable environment that fosters positive interactions. It becomes easier to build rapport, trust, and meaningful connections, setting the stage for cooperative projects, intimate conversations, and valuable life moments.

For me, cooking brings this to the surface quite tangibly. I can't even begin to chop an onion unless the kitchen is first in order, because a messy kitchen clutters my mind, throws off my rhythm and makes the entire process inefficient and downright unpleasant. So, my cooking ritual always begins with tidying up. By the time I've laid out all my ingredients and cooking tools, the kitchen is already in a state that brings clarity and focus.

As I prepare my meals, I continue this practice of cleanliness. Utensils are washed as soon as they've served their purpose, spices are immediately returned to their rightful place, and waste is promptly discarded. What might look like multitasking is actually a seamless flow that makes the whole process not just efficient, but deeply satisfying. And when it's all said and done, I'm left with a week's worth of meals, each portioned perfectly, on the benchtop of a kitchen that's cleaner than when I started. This isn't just about the convenience of having meals ready for the week; it's about the deep sense of satisfaction that comes from maintaining an environment that allows me to function at my best. It's like a cycle of self-respect: I respect my space, which in turn enables me to produce something wonderful, reinforcing my sense of self-respect.

Small wonder cleanliness and organisation go hand in hand with success. Your surroundings act as a tangible mirror reflecting your inner emotional and mental state. A cluttered space often indicates a cluttered mind and provides the right conditions for a cascading effect of setbacks and failures. When things aren't going your way, a good place to start, if you wish to turn your luck around, is to clean your home, starting with the room where you spend the most time — likely the bedroom or your home office. Tidying your environment is the first step towards reclaiming agency over your life.

I bet you brush your teeth when you wake up in the morning, but do you also make your bed? This simple ritual sets the tone for the rest of the day. You've accomplished one task, and you're ready for the next. The state of your home and workspace isn't a frivolous detail; it's an indicator of self-respect that will command admiration and respect from those around you. And should your day still suck despite going through all this effort, wouldn't things get better if you're welcomed home by a clean environment and a bed that is made?

Don't underestimate the domino effect of these actions, no matter how small. Over time, they don't just build a pattern; they become part of your brand. They build a lifestyle, an image, and a level of self-respect that sets the stage for everything else you aim to achieve.

Criticism: A Bus That's Never Late
While your efforts to keep yourself and your environment in check offer incalculable benefits, they can also make you a target for criticism and unsolicited psychoanalysis. It's not uncommon to hear snide remarks or armchair diagnoses thrown your way, branding you as "neurotic," or even slapping clinical terms like "OCD" and "narcissism" onto your lifestyle choices. These criticisms are often devoid of any real understanding of what these terms mean, and they're usually lobbed by individuals who have little interest in elevating their own lives.

The price we pay for striving to be better is a life where we perpetually find ourselves in the crosshairs of those who relish in mediocrity. And as much as it stings to face such criticism, especially when you're making earnest efforts to improve, it's just one of those things you'll have to learn to tolerate to a degree. Yet, even in these instances, there's a silver lining; an antidote to such criticism. It is to surround yourself with the right people—those who appreciate the value of self-respect, who understand the difference between constructive feedback and baseless judgment. So, when you find yourself bombarded with misplaced labels or derisive comments, use them as a filter. This criticism inadvertently performs a service for you: it exposes the individuals whose value in your life is a net negative, making it easier for you to distance yourself from them. It's like they're doing the hard work of vetting your social circle for you, revealing who should and shouldn't be a part of your journey towards becoming a better person, one step at a time.

The Ripple Effect
If you're wondering what the connection is between dressing well, staying fit and being tidy, the answer is simple: self-respect. Every action we take, from the clothes we choose to the way we present our living spaces, forms a composite image of who we are and how we value ourselves. These aren't isolated acts; they're interconnected facets of a lifestyle rooted in self-worth. When we stand up straight, with our shoulders back, garbed in clothes that reflect our best selves, inhabiting spaces that are as clean and ordered as they are inviting, we're making a statement to the world—and, more importantly, to ourselves, that we are worthy.

We become what we project, so why not project the best version of ourselves? It's not about being disingenuous or artificial; it's about making our best selves the default setting. The more consistent you are in maintaining these good habits, the more they become ingrained in your character. Eventually, it won't even feel like effort; it will simply be who you are.

If you ever struggle keeping up with these habits, especially when you're feeling down, remember the importance of resilience and adaptability. We talked about this earlier, and it holds true here as well. Just like in weightlifting, where the last few reps are the ones that count the most, the real test of your character is how you maintain your standards under pressure. The world won't always make it easy for you, but the real victory lies in upholding your values even when conforming to what's convenient in the moment would be the easier thing to do.

My message here is straightforward: respect yourself, and others will follow. Elevate your standards, nurture your body, cherish your space, and cultivate a life where self-respect is the norm, not the exception. As you forge ahead in your journey through life, my hope is that you'll keep this lesson close to your heart. Know that in respecting yourself, you're laying down a foundation of self-love and self-worth that can't easily be shaken. And that, my dear, is a legacy worth striving for, both for yourself and for those lucky enough to be a part of your life.

*"True ignorance is not the absence of knowledge,
but the refusal to acquire it."*
Karl Popper

Cultivate a Growth Mindset: Turn Learning Into a Hobby

To be able to live a life with purpose and thrive throughout your ambitious pursuits, it is essential to cultivate a growth mindset. This means learning to accept challenges as opportunities for personal development. I know it's easier said than done, but when you encounter obstacles, try reframing the situation to see them as stepping stones—each filled with lessons for achieving your goals—helping you become a stronger and more grounded person in the process.

Harness the Power of Incremental Change
I encourage you to practice the Japanese philosophy of Kaizen. It's a method for continuous improvement that involves making small, incremental changes that, when observed in isolation, may seem inconsequential. But as tiny as these adjustments might look to the untrained eye, when compounded, they lead to profound improvements over time. Imagine the changing of the seasons in nature or a young oak tree that grows a little taller every day. Initially, you may not notice much difference, but as time passes,

the entire landscape changes, and as the tree matures, it becomes a towering presence. Similarly, you could turn your journey through life into a long series of small, consistent efforts that accumulate into remarkable achievements.

Picture yourself learning a new language (I know a thing or two about this). Rather than overwhelming yourself with vocabulary lists and grammar rules from the get-go, take it one word at a time, then one sentence at a time. Today, learn to say "hello," and tomorrow, learn to say "how are you?" By the end of the month, you'll be able to introduce yourself and even make small talk. That's Kaizen. Your day-by-day improvement is almost laughable, but when you look back, you'll be amazed at how far you've come.

Gamification In Action
Think about high school for a moment. Did you ever have a tough subject—like physics, chemistry or calculus—that felt like a mountain you could never climb? I want you to look at such hurdles as if you're a rock climber. At first glance, the mountain may seem daunting. But for a rock climber, each crevice or ledge becomes an opportunity—a way to climb higher. That's the growth mindset in action. It tells you that with every problem, there's a solution tucked away somewhere, and that you have what it takes to discover it.

The key to enjoying this process and turning it into a habit is to gamify it. Yes, turn learning into a game. It doesn't have to be a drag or a chore. Reward yourself for solving a difficult equation or for finishing a challenging book. This approach doesn't just make learning fun; it makes it addictive. Don't believe me? Ask your mother if I ever stopped reaching for the next milestone or if I ever quit something simply because it got too hard.

Once you adopt this mindset, you too will find yourself continually looking for the next challenge because you'll know that it's another opportunity to grow. Perhaps you no longer remember how we'd celebrate when you completed a puzzle, solved a math problem or used a new word when you were little, but it's the same thing. Those rewards make your brain associate learning with pleasure, and soon enough, you're not just doing it because you have to; you're doing it because you want to, because it's fun.

Adopt Technology, But Don't Be Its Slave
As you introduce new technology into your way of life, don't let it dictate how you live or what you believe. I want you to learn, my child, to become watchful, to be resourceful, and to rely on facts over opinions. In this post-truth era where news is mostly propaganda, maintaining a healthy level of scepticism should be your default response when exposed to the media. And if a topic matters to you, do your own research.

Technology has been a game-changer in my lifetime, and my generation has enjoyed a front-row seat to the digital revolution. From the genesis of the modern internet and the debut of the first smart phone to the rise of self-driving cars and the explosion of artificial intelligence, I've not only witnessed but felt its transformative impact. It's reshaped our lives, turbocharged our potential, and connected us in unimaginable ways—a blessing in an ever-changing world.

For me, technology has been a complex companion. It played a crucial role in rekindling my relationship with your mother after I moved away, and it was later instrumental in our decision to make a life in Australia. Despite its benefits, however, it's still a double-edged sword.

Your generation will experience levels of automation and manipulation that I don't even want to imagine, so make sure you always evaluate the information presented to you, for technology has the power to liberate or enslave depending on how much of our freewill we surrender to it. The choice will ultimately be yours. I trust you'll make the right one.

But don't be a luddite either! Like fire, technology has the power to sustain life or destroy it. It's your responsibility to learn to use it to your benefit without getting burned.

Technology will become an integral part of your world far more than it was in mine, so be curious and try to understand how it works, not necessarily from a technical perspective, but from a sociological one. How does it change how we behave and communicate? How does it impact the way we feel? How does it influence what we believe? To answer these types of questions, you'll need to cultivate your critical thinking and you'll also need to get used to checking your sources.

Lean on the wisdom of mentors and loved ones, as well as literature, history, and yes, even technology itself, for it offers endless opportunities for learning and personal development. Whether you choose online courses, interactive apps or forums where you can share and gather knowledge from artificial intelligence chatbots or other humans, the digital age can significantly boost your learning potential and speed. But I must warn you—don't let it run your life. It's easy to become addicted to our devices, giving up more and more of our agency to technocrat puppeteers who don't have our best interests at heart. Lower your guard and, before you know it, you'll have stopped thinking for yourself. So always remember: Learn to control the technology you use, for it will never tire of trying to control you.

Beyond Degrees

"The value of a college education is that it trains the mind to think. And that's something you can't learn from textbooks." This quote, generally attributed to Albert Einstein, resonates strongly with me because going to business school reignited my thirst for knowledge, setting me on a path to further education, completing a second post-graduate degree and earning various other qualifications. This journey didn't just enhance my professional value; it turned me into a more well-rounded individual because it expanded my knowledge in diverse domains, from philosophy to technology and everything in between.

Find Your Terminal Velocity

The moment you were born, I felt an overwhelming sense of duty—like I hit a gear I didn't even know I had. I've always been proactive, but your tiny presence turbocharged my ambition with an overwhelming sense of responsibility. Nothing's been able to slow me down since. One of my old mates, having witnessed this change of pace, asked me for my secret sauce. I told him that it's a combination of knowing your destination, committing to the journey, and staying agile enough to be able to change direction and adapt to changing conditions along the way. When he reminded me that we were not at work, I said, "Assume responsibility for your own destiny and prioritise what you do based on value, not comfort." So there it is, sweetheart, my nugget of wisdom now passed on to you.

Now, let's talk tactics. I highly recommend that you set up a kanban board for your learning journey. Queue up your books, courses, and seminars so that each one builds on the last. That's what I do and it's no state secret—it's just good old project management. But remember, planning gets you nowhere without action. I've set aside several hours each week for focused effort, and that's kept me within arm's reach of every major milestone I've set. Whether it's personal or professional, the process is the same. That said, don't think that I've got every second of my day earmarked for some grand scheme. I leave plenty of "me" time, and that's when the magic happens. When I give myself the freedom to just be, that's when my best ideas pop up and my most meaningful work gets done, and this is not by chance, my dear; it's a vital part of how I stay productive.

Some people opt for the slow burn of a marathon, while others sprint until they're spent, but I prefer the train method. Like a train, it takes an initial burst of hard work to set me in motion, but once I gain momentum, I'm practically unstoppable. I call this my "Terminal Velocity"—the maximum pace I can sustain over the long haul.

Once you nail down your own terminal velocity, you'll be astounded by how precisely you can forecast the time and effort needed to hit your milestones. But remember, maintaining top speed indefinitely isn't viable; there's always the drag factor and the risk of depleting your fuel. Speed might be exciting, but it's useless if you can't go the distance. So, before setting out, get crystal clear about your end goal, the sacrifices you're willing to make, and how you'll navigate detours, whether it's life getting in the way or saboteurs distracting you from your mission.

What enables me to sustain a pace that many consider "unsustainable" is that I understand that I don't need to maintain it forever—it's just until I reach my destination. And when you have clarity about where you're headed, the distance to cover, and what you're willing to trade off to get there, the journey may not necessarily get easier, but it does become simpler.

I've yet to meet a high achiever who credits their success to the practice of moderation or taking things easy. On the contrary, they often cite focus, perseverance, and grit. I'm prepared for the trade-offs required to meet my lofty goals. You may find an easier path, but if yours looks anything like mine, the higher you aim, the greater the sacrifices you must be willing to make.

The MBA Advantage

Completing an MBA is akin to applying the Kaizen method on a grand scale. As you progress through the curriculum, your knowledge and understanding gradually increase, preparing you for even more complex subjects. Soon enough, you become fluent in business management, finance, psychology, and more. But the benefits don't end at graduation, since your newfound skills will continually elevate your professional contributions to any organisation you choose to work for, or even your own.

Now, I don't want you to think that learning occurs solely within the confines of a classroom. That's a long way from the truth. However, structured education, like an MBA, provides a unique learning setting. It equips you with a broad range of skills, transforming you into an "A" player no matter your career choice. Whether you aim to lead a team, manage a non-profit, or even launch your own company, the wisdom gained from a well-crafted program is invaluable. Simply learning the jargon and becoming comfortable with it already gives you a significant edge.

An MBA enables you to better understand the role of people and technology in business and society. It arms you with the skills to distinguish between good innovations and those that drain your energy, and places you in an environment filled with ambitious individuals seeking to become a better version of themselves. We'll revisit this point in the chapter, "Choose Your Family: Bond with Purpose."

Darling, I can't stress enough how transformative this experience was for me; it split my life into before and after. I highly encourage you to broaden your perspectives and expand your horizons by enrolling in a top business school. Trust your daddy, you won't regret it.

An MBA Is Like Karate

The road towards earning an MBA is similar to the one that earns you a black belt. It renders you more resourceful and resilient, but only in exchange for your full commitment and an unwavering degree of discipline.

As you ascend through the ranks, compete in tournaments and learn how to take a hit, many whose opinions you once valued will claim that what you're doing won't work in the real world. Despite this, your commitment never wavers, because you know that if you stay the course, you'll master the techniques that will empower you to lead with confidence, to perform well under pressure, and to earn the kind of respect that only comes from a strong foundation coupled with experience. And should you ever find yourself in a high-stakes situation, your practical knowledge will automatically kick in like a reflex.

In disciplines like Karate and Tang Soo Do, earning a black belt does not mark the end, but rather the beginning of your journey. Others might think you've arrived, but you'll know all too well that you're just getting started. At that point, your early detractors will stare in awe as you surpass them, and when they face similar challenges, they'll freeze, pondering what could have been if only they had trained like you did.

Learning: An Infinite Game

We've covered a lot here, from how to tackle challenges and improve continuously, to the pros and cons of using technology and the benefits of attending business school. But the key takeaway is simple: Never stop learning. Cultivating a growth mindset is an ongoing process, and each day offers new opportunities for betterment. Whether you are absorbing knowledge from a book, a class, or even a casual conversation, every experience offers you an opportunity to become more knowledgeable and, eventually, wiser.

People often ask me why I keep collecting qualifications. After all, I've already reached a point where attaining more won't necessarily lead to fancier job titles or a bigger salary. During chemotherapy, some of my well-meaning friends were worried and even suggested that I may have gone insane because I kept studying despite the apparent futility of it all—likely because they thought I was in denial. But they were all missing the point then and many of them still are. I do what I do not just to pad my résumé. It's about practising what I preach; about embodying resilience not just in my words but in my actions. It's about setting a positive example for you. Besides, in a world where the pace of change is accelerating, if you're not moving forward, you're falling behind.

Where do I get my motivation? Well, for starters, I don't go looking for it because chasing motivation is a fool's errand. Motivation is a distraction, and willpower is a limited resource that I cannot do without, so I don't waste it by searching for mind hacks. That's like trying to make yourself hungry when you should be out finding food. Instead, I come up with systems. I nurture positive behaviours. I focus on setting achievable milestones that progressively help me reach my goals.

That's where I invest most of my effort; first on finding out what it is I really want and then on breaking it down into smaller, more sensible targets that, collectively, build up to my biggest goals. Sometimes I run, sometimes I crawl, sometimes I pivot, but progress is progress and that's what matters. Time often takes care of the rest.

So, baby, never underestimate the power of continuous learning. It keeps you sharp, opens new doors, and empowers you to face life's toughest challenges with courage and hope. Stay curious, because when you dig into what you think you already know, you often realise just how much more you have yet to discover. Cultivating a growth mindset isn't just a good idea; it's a fundamental building block for your ambitions and your pursuit of greatness. In short, keep your eyes open, nurture your hunger for knowledge, and turn learning into a lifelong hobby—because when it comes to growing and learning, the game never ends.

> *"The better ambitions have to do with the development of character and ability, rather than status and power. Status you can lose. [But] you carry character with you wherever you go, and it allows you to prevail."*
> Jordan Peterson

Nurture Your Ambition: Strive for Greatness

Ambition is a powerful force that, when nurtured with purpose, discipline, and perseverance, can lead to greatness. And "greatness" is not an end but a continuous journey of growth and improvement. You'll often hear that ambition is bad, but let's not confuse it with greed. Ambition is good; greed is bad. Ambition is a benefit; greed is a burden. Ambition propels you forward; greed drags you down. Ambition breeds prosperity; greed breeds misery.

Use your ambition like a tool; a compass to direct you towards your dreams and aspirations. But be mindful of dreams, my dear, for they are full of fallacies and incongruencies that will not be obvious to you while you're still half asleep. Understanding their logic, what might have sparked them, and why you've decided to chase them are only the first steps.

Be ambitious with your goals but understand why you're setting them in the first place. When you define something that you want, ask yourself why you want it. When you get your answer, ask again. Do it five times and be specific. You'll often find that your original goal was just a stepping-stone or merely one of many potential paths towards achieving your primary aim. Defining your true north sets you free from spinning your wheels trying to reach pointless milestones or becoming fixated on tearing down walls when a door might be wide open right in front of you.

Defining Your Ambitions

Imagine goals as destinations on a map, and your ambition as the journey. Setting goals is important, but it's not enough. You must ask yourself why each goal matters to you, and when you understand the true purpose behind them, it will fuel your ambition with direction and meaning.

Setting goals is like planning a trip. If you don't get started and haven't planned how to get there, you'll never reach your destination. Ambition requires hard work, planning, and determination. It's not about writing wish lists or "manifesting" your wants into existence—whatever that means. It's about being proactive and making things happen because goal setting is not magical.

Goals without execution are nothing but dreams, and execution without planning and risk management is both reckless and dumb. You may get lucky sometimes and still achieve a lot despite your poor execution, but relying on good luck to achieve anything in life is a fool's tactic. Don't be a fool. Work hard on identifying your strengths, your weaknesses, your privileges and disadvantages, and learn to use them to get ahead, because as much as I love you . . .

You Are Not Special

That's right. I could stroke your ego and tell you that you can be anything and achieve everything you set your mind to, but that's not what you need from your father. Life is not fair, and not a single law of physics states that people get what they deserve.

Every day, good people get dealt bad hands and bad people get dealt straight flushes. It happens. It's not fair. Get used to it. Whinging about it, painting your fingernails black or becoming a nihilist will get you nowhere, especially when so few things in life will ever be under your direct control. Instead of dwelling on this unfairness, try to focus on what you can influence—your decisions and actions—because success is not just about reaching your goals; it's also about the choices you make and the effort you put in along the way. Accepting that the game is rigged, understanding its rules, and learning when to follow and when to bend them is what will give you a winning edge in life; the edge commonly referred to as "good luck."

Good luck is nothing but the compounded result of a series of harmonious events, often sparked by a long streak of good decisions. The frequency and quality of the decisions you make will ultimately determine the amount of good luck that you will experience in life. So, become the primary decision-maker throughout your journey, as luck favours those who are prepared and proactive. Once people begin to attribute your achievements to good luck, you'll have all the evidence you'll need to know that you've been playing your cards right. Such comments may sting when you first hear them, but in time, you'll learn to welcome them, because becoming the recipient of this kind of cynicism helps you cull your inner circle from detractors so you can give your ever-growing network of net promoters more of the space that they rightfully deserve.

Self-awareness, as discussed earlier, is crucial on this journey. Understand your strengths and weaknesses and use them strategically. Recognise your privileges and disadvantages and acquire the skills to leverage them. Your self-awareness will help you map your route, guiding you through life's twists and turns.

Striving for Greatness

I have good news for you; greatness is subjective. That means you decide what it means to you, and only you can deliberate on whether you've achieved it. You are your own judge and I will not burden you with my expectations of what you should be or do with your life. To me, you've already become everything I ever hoped you'd be. You are my daughter, and being your father helped me achieve my own greatness. What I will ask you is to strive for greatness too, however you choose to define it, because doing so not only elevates you but also makes you deserving of the life and privileges you've been given.

Nurture Your Ambition

Like a fire that burns within you, ambition urges you to grow and expand your horizons. And as you learn to take control of your life, your ambition will become your most trusted ally in achieving your dreams. But remember, life is a marathon, not a sprint, so greatness is not achieved overnight. Rather, it is the result of consistent effort and a lifelong commitment to do better.

Inevitably, there will be times when you face setbacks and your resolve is challenged. It is during these moments that your determination and resilience will come into play. Remember that navigating through life is not about avoiding obstacles; it's about having the grit to overcome them. Think of each setback as a test; a chance to renew your commitment to your goals and to yourself. It's natural to feel discouraged when life gets difficult, but don't let this stop you. Every setback can be a stepping stone to success if you approach it with the right mindset. So, collect yourself, get focused, and keep going, as these moments often present the best opportunities to learn and grow.

For example, in Greece, it took me years to leave the past behind and let go of what I had lost, but in time, I learned to appreciate what I had gained — the ability to be present and the freedom to not be bounded by extraneous expectations that prevented me from focusing on what really mattered to me in life. So, don't forget to appreciate the present moment. Life forms a mosaic of tiny experiences, and sometimes, the most beautiful patterns emerge unexpectedly. Welcome spontaneity, cherish your relationships, and find joy in the simple pleasures of life, for it isn't just about personal success; it's also about making a positive impact in the world and in the lives of the people around you.

As you progress through life, keep in mind that every achievement, big or small, is a step towards something greater. So, take a moment to appreciate your effort, as well as the love and support you receive as you cross each milestone. These incremental steps are the building blocks of your ambition, and they set the foundation you'll need to support your future.

Systems Eat Goals for Breakfast
To make your ambition work for you, consider developing systems instead of just setting goals. A system is a structured approach to improve consistency in your efforts to achieve your objectives. It involves breaking down your goals into smaller,

more manageable steps and creating a process to follow with dedication and discipline. This approach is not only practical, but sustainable.

Consider this example: Rather than setting a one-year deadline to write a novel, you can establish a systematic approach. Allocate specific days for writing and research and separate days for feedback and editing. Systematic approaches like these ensure that you make steady progress and increase your chances of success, even when the goal may still seem distant or unattainable. Alternatively, if you instead focus solely on the deadline, you are more likely to waste time when the date is far and become overwhelmed when it's coming closer. This once again strikes at the heart of Kaizen, as these incremental improvements, over time, will compound to deliver significant results.

Discipline: Life's Greatest Hack

The key to achieving anything worthwhile is discipline. It helps you create and maintain momentum, and it keeps you focused. It's easy to get distracted by the constant noise and demands of life. But discipline helps you stay on track. It's the ability to prioritise your goals and make the necessary trade-offs to achieve them. Discipline takes you to the gym when you don't feel like training, it gets you out of bed when you'd rather sleep in, and it keeps your mouth shut when all you want is to scream. Discipline is what separates those who bend life to their will from those who just wait for life to happen—those who do nothing but whine when things don't go their way.

Create routines and habits that resonate with your ambitions. These might involve dedicating focused time to your studies, workouts, meal preparation, or managing your investments. Remember, consistency holds the key.

Be Mindful of Your Social Circle

I must stress that the company you keep can either fuel your determination or hinder your progress. Choose companions and mentors who either share your values and ambition, who support and inspire you, or who at least cheer you on along the way. If all this aligns, you've hit the jackpot.

Keep in mind that you will inevitably become the average of the people you spend the most time with, so be mindful of who you bring into your circle because success is a team sport. Surround yourself with a support network that believes in you and wants you to succeed. Reach out to coaches and advisors who can provide guidance and encouragement, share your aspirations with loved ones who can offer emotional support during tough moments, and seek guidance and advice from mentors who have walked a similar path or who have progressed beyond it. Look up to them and learn all you can. Their wisdom can be invaluable in shaping your own journey and in teaching you new ways to uplift and inspire those who look up to you.

Your ambition mirrors your potential; think of it as a tree you've planted in your backyard. You now have the responsibility to care for it. And as you sow the seeds of your ambition, ponder how your actions can enrich the lives of others. When your journey is fuelled by purpose and guided by values like empathy, kindness, and love, it possesses the remarkable power to not only transform your life but also to leave a positive imprint on those around you. This is a privilege and you must regard it with the respect it deserves.

Redefining Failure

Failures are common byproducts of every ambitious journey, but this isn't necessarily a sign of inadequacy. Most of the time, it's just a matter of chance. Nevertheless, every setback can teach you valuable lessons to strengthen your resolve. You may not particularly enjoy dirt, but if you like hiking, you'd better get used to it. And if the trail didn't have dirt, then it would just be a road and you wouldn't call it hiking.

Perseverance, like resilience, can be a powerful ally during hard times. When faced with obstacles, remind yourself of your purpose and the value of your ambitions. It's the willingness to endure hardships that distinguishes those who achieve greatness from those who settle for mediocrity.

Setting Expectations
To achieve anything worthwhile, you must be willing to make sacrifices. These trade-offs are inevitable on the road to achieving personal success.

There's a metaphor in project management known as "The Iron Triangle" that illustrates this point beautifully. It starts as an equilateral triangle where the top corner is labelled "time", the right corner "cost", and the left corner "scope". The inside of the triangle is labelled "quality".

Suppose you have a project where a given stage was overrun due to some unforeseen challenge. You now have three options to keep the project alive:

a) You could extend the schedule, and while that wouldn't necessarily lower quality, it would increase your costs.
b) You could reduce the scope to keep the schedule on track, but then you'd no longer deliver what the project intended.
c) You could cut corners and shift resources to still finish on track and on budget, but then you'd be sacrificing quality and scope.

In other words, you can have everything, but not at the same time. This applies to life as well. To attain anything you want, you need to identify what you must give up in order to get it. Never assume that you can have "it" all whenever you want. That's childish, narcissistic... and impossible. So, be realistic in the expectations you set for yourself and those you set for others, because we are terrible at estimating time and effort. Our human tendency is to overestimate what we can achieve over one year, and by the same token, we grossly underestimate what we can achieve in three, five, and ten years. It would be, therefore, wise for you to accept that achieving your goals in life will not happen overnight, as doing so is often the result of years of dedication and hard work. But if you stay committed to your purpose and remain agile enough to adapt and pivot as needed, you will eventually enjoy the fruits of your labour.

Change is Inevitable
Life is a remarkable journey filled with twists and turns, isn't it? Change, my dear, will be your ever-faithful companion on this path. How do you plan to welcome it with an open heart and a flexible mindset, knowing that life rarely unfolds exactly as we imagine? You'll be faced with many challenges and opportunities, but never let hesitation or worse yet, indecision, make the next move for you. The act of not making a choice is a choice in itself, so make your own moves, and if things don't work out like you hoped, that's ok. These experiences will then become lessons that help you evolve into someone stronger, wiser and better prepared than you were yesterday.

As you progress through your journey, remember to face your challenges in stride and draw wisdom from moments of failure. These experiences will serve as compass points guiding you forward. How do you envision your ambitions evolving, your goals shifting, and the person you'll grow into as you shape the path ahead?

Balancing Ambition and Contentment

As your father, I encourage you to dream big, to work hard, and to never lose confidence in your ability to achieve your aspirations. With the right mindset, good discipline and unfettered determination, you have the potential to make a meaningful impact on the world and leave a legacy worthy of your intentions. But don't make a habit of setting absurdly ambitious goals, for this can blind you from seeing the more attainable opportunities that may be right in front of you; the ones that can realistically help you fulfil your purpose and find contentment.

Every achievement, big or small, is a step towards something greater. The satisfaction I felt upon reaching each of our lofty milestones was not just about achieving a self-imposed arbitrary measure of success; it was about finishing what I started, about absorbing the lessons, and about recognising the love of those who supported me throughout the journey.

While ambition is a driving force, it's essential to strike a balance between your aspirations and contentment with the present. Ambition should fuel your desire to improve and achieve more, yet it should never overshadow your appreciation of the present. Take moments to pause and reflect on your journey. Celebrate not only your triumphs but also the people who have supported you, the lessons you've learned, and the experiences that have shaped you, for you can use that as fuel for the next leg of your journey.

I'd be lying if I said I've achieved every goal I've set for myself. And I'm glad I haven't. Had I always gotten my way, I never would have left home, and that would have been a disappointing waste of a life well lived. That's why I say that success is not a destination, but a continuous journey, and "greatness" is not a static or even tangible state, but a dynamic process; one of growth and intentional improvement. And if I were to rate myself against my childhood expectations of where I would have liked to be today, I'm happy to report that I would rate my life project on time and on budget. My ambition and contentment are in balance at last.

Try to find joy in the present and be grateful for the path you've walked and for those who've joined you, for in the end, your greatness will not be measured by your personal achievements but by the positive impact you had on those who walked alongside you, those you carried, and those who carried you.

Your Path is Unique . . . but Shared
Seek inspiration from mentors, role models, and the wisdom of others, but remember that your journey is uniquely yours. As such, you must rely on your individuality, trust your instincts, and make sure that your ambitions reflect your own values, passions, and dreams. Don't let societal expectations or the desires of others dictate your path. Always be true to yourself and your vision.

However, as you pursue your own greatness, remember that your journey has the power to inspire, so take every available opportunity to help someone up. Your determination, kindness, and commitment can serve as motivation for those around you, but make sure that your ambitions do not come at their expense. Instead, they should contribute to the betterment of society. For this reason, I'd encourage you to document your experiences because, with humility and authenticity, sharing both the good and the bad won't embarrass you; rather, it will elevate you.

Acknowledging your setbacks and the lessons you've learned are not only the hallmarks of a great leader, but it helps you connect with others who face similar obstacles, so that together, you can rise and grow stronger.

I am profoundly proud of the remarkable little person that you are today and the boundless potential you carry within. As you begin to set your ambitions, let them be guided by purpose, discipline, and a commitment to positive values. Keep your heart open to growth, your mind receptive to learning, and your spirit resilient in the face of challenges, for your journey towards greatness is neither a path that you'll walk alone nor one that can only benefit you. It's a legacy that you can leave behind, and if you document it, an inspiration for future generations.

"Compound interest is the greatest invention in human history. He who understands it, earns it; he who doesn't, pays it."
Unknown

Learn Finance: Master Cash Flow and Compounding

The great stoic, Epictetus, posited that "Wealth consists not in having great possessions, but in having few wants." One could interpret this wisdom as a call to develop apathy towards financial prosperity, but I see it differently. While I agree with the overall statement, I've learned that the key to having few wants is having enough. Enough to be independent, enough to care for yourself and your loved ones, enough to determine how you spend your very limited time on this Earth. If any of these conditions is lacking, your mind will be clouded by endless wants devised by your lizard brain to distract you from the pain that would otherwise paralyse you.

Master the Basics
You've probably heard a million times that "Money doesn't grow on trees." This wealth limiting phrase serves as a cautionary tale about the importance of being careful with money. But here's a twist—while money may not grow on trees, it can grow. The key to making it grow lies in understanding some basic financial

principles: cash flow, leveraging, debt management, and the power of compounding.

Cash Flow: The Lifeblood of Your Finances

Imagine cash flow as the circulatory system of your financial body. In a living organism, the heart pumps blood to various parts, ensuring life and vitality. Similarly, cash flow refers to how money moves in and out of your life. There's income (your heart), expenses (your body parts consuming resources), and the blood vessels are your various accounts and investments. Just like a healthy circulatory system, a positive cash flow ensures that you can meet your needs and even save or invest for the future.

The Art of Leveraging

Leveraging is a term you might hear often in the realm of finance. It's the practice of using borrowed money for investment and earning a return greater than the interest payable. Think of it as "lifting heavy financial weights" using the strength of your assets and creditworthiness, not just your muscles. Does this sound overly complicated? Don't stress. It's not, and it's particularly useful when investing in big-ticket items like property. More on that later.

Debt: A Double-Edged Sword

Contrary to popular belief, debt isn't always bad. Sure, it's not ideal to be drowning in credit card bills, but some types of debt can be beneficial. Good debt is an investment that will grow in value or generate long-term income, like getting a mortgage for an investment-grade residential property that you'll rent out to a tenant. We call this an "asset," because it makes money for you.

Bad debt, on the other hand, is borrowing for something that depreciates in value and does not generate an income, like the latest tech gadget or, more notably, a jet ski. In both cases, your purchase won't help you build wealth, and in the case of the jet ski, it will also increase your ongoing costs for as long as you own it. We call this a "liability," because it's something that costs you money.

The Power of Compounding

Compounding is the financial world's equivalent of the snowball effect, but this isn't just any snowball—it's one made of money. Imagine rolling a snowball down a hill; with each roll, it gathers more snow and gets bigger. Now, replace the snow it picks up with interest earned on your initial investment. The more time you give it, the more it rolls, the more interest it gathers, and the wealthier you become.

At its core, compounding involves earning interest on your initial investment, and then earning interest on that interest, and so on. To make this magic happen, you need two things: time and reinvestment. Time allows your investments to grow, and reinvesting your earnings can turbocharge that growth. Let's bring this to life with an example.

Mary, the Early Bird: Starts investing $10,000 per annum from the age of 20 until she turns 30. After that, she doesn't invest another dollar. That's a total investment of $100,000 over 10 years.

Tim, the Late Starter: Invests the same $10,000 annually, but starts at the age of 30 and continues to do so until he retires at 60. He invests a total of $300,000 over 30 years.

Both investors receive a consistent annual return of 10%. But by the time they reach the age of 60, Mary, who only invested for 10 years, would have amassed around $1,863,000. Tim, on the other hand, who invested three times as much money over a 30-year period, would end up with approximately $1,745,000. That's well over $100,000 poorer.

Intriguingly, Tim, who invested three times more money than Mary did, ends up with less simply because he started later. The stark difference between these two outcomes is purely due to the compounding effect, which favours time in the market over the size of the investment.

This is far more than textbook theory — it's a fundamental principle that works just as well in real life. Understanding this, and doing something about it, can significantly influence the course of your life, the course of your children's lives, and if you do well, the course of your grandchildren's lives.

So, what's the lesson here? The lesson is to start early, to be consistent, and whether you choose to invest in property, stocks or both, to let compounding do its work.

These are the building blocks of financial literacy. I hope this lesson wasn't too overwhelming. My aim here is to give you the basics, making the complicated world of finance slightly more accessible — and hopefully, more interesting. Armed with this knowledge, you'll be better equipped to continue your education so you can start making your own financial moves. Speaking of moves — and assuming you're now in your twenties — you're likely wondering whether it's better to invest in property or stocks, aren't you?

Property vs Stocks: A Tale of Two Investments

1. Residential Property: The Aussie Dream

The Great Australian Dream has long been about owning your own home. And for good reason! Residential property in our largest cities has been a solid investment for decades. Why? Well, a combination of a growing population, strict zoning laws stifling new construction, and a chronic undersupply of government funded social housing keeps driving up property values.

The property market is often considered less volatile than the stock market. Additionally, banks are usually quite willing to lend a significant amount to property buyers, often allowing leverage of 10 to 20 times your initial investment. At its most fundamental level, this amplifies your exposure.

To break this down with an example, say you've saved $100,000 for a deposit. You can now leverage this amount to secure a one-million-dollar property by getting a mortgage from a bank with a 90% loan to value ratio (LVR). In this case, your $100,000 deposit has given you control of a one-million-dollar asset—that's 10x leverage.

Now, imagine that the property market goes up by 10% the following year. Your property is now worth $1.1 million. If you sold it at this price—let's ignore taxes and fees for now—you'd make a $100,000 profit on top of your initial $100,000 investment. This translates to a 100% return, even though the property's value only increased by 10%. That's the power of leverage at work. However, the reverse is also true, and while leverage can amplify your gains, it can also amplify your losses. So tread carefully and do your homework.

2. Index Funds: The Quiet Achiever

Now, let's discuss index funds. Imagine you're craving some fruit, but instead of buying a kilo of apples, you buy a one-kilo fruit salad with diced apples, oranges, bananas, and berries. This is called diversification. An index fund works similarly, as it tracks a market index such as the S&P 500, which includes 500 of the largest U.S. companies by market capitalisation. Rather than selecting individual stocks and hoping that they rise, you're now investing in a broad segment of the market. This is a wise strategy because statistical evidence shows it's extremely difficult for individual investors to consistently outperform the market over time. Therefore, index funds can offer a safer and more reliable way to increase your wealth, particularly if you're not comfortable exploring other investment options.

Over the past few decades, investing in this index—either through an index fund or an exchange-traded fund (ETF)—has returned an average of 10% per annum. So, if you invested the same $100,000 that you used for the property, your total profit after one year would be $10,000 (not $100,000). Does this make property a better investment? Not exactly. That's because both options yielded the same 10% return on your investment. What caused the stark difference in your total profit was that with the property, you had 10x leverage. Moreover, a bank is far more willing to issue a loan backed by a tangible asset like residential property than one backed by stocks because stocks are a much riskier asset class.

Leverage: The Game-Changer

While property and stocks both have their merits, the most significant advantage that one can have over the other lies in the power of leverage. As we just covered, getting a 10-20x loan from a bank for a property purchase is far more feasible than getting one to purchase a basket of stocks. The main reason property is more likely to yield exponential gains is primarily because you're controlling a much larger asset, and you're doing so with the bank's money. It's like activating a cheat code—it may seem shifty, but in this case, it's all part of the game.

Why Not Both?

After building a strong property portfolio, you might find yourself sitting on a goldmine of equity. But property has its downsides too—low rental returns, dealing with tenants, and ongoing maintenance costs. This is when diversifying into index funds could come into play, turning your "bricks and mortar" wealth into a more liquid, high-return investment at a later age.

For example, imagine you're in your late 40s or early 50s. You own properties worth a total of $5 million, but they only bring in a modest 2.5% net return based on their value. This would equate to a yearly income of $125,000 after accounting for rent and all property-related expenses. But say you liquidated, paid 25% in capital gains tax, and ended up with a net profit of $4 million. In this scenario, you could invest $3 million in an index fund like the S&P 500 and, theoretically, you'd end up with a yearly income of $300,000. You'd also get to keep a healthy $1 million cash buffer to cover for years when your index fund experiences below average returns. And did I mention this income is completely hands off? No more tenants, no more costly evictions, and no more maintenance requests. It's retirement income the way it's meant to be. But barring receiving a huge windfall in your 20s or becoming a highly successful entrepreneur, the most common strategy to get to this point, in our side of the world, begins with your first investment property.

In short, if you're aiming to build wealth from scratch, investing in property is often the most direct route. However, once you've amassed enough equity, it usually makes sense to liquidate your portfolio and reinvest your proceeds into stocks. Not only are their dividends and capital appreciation more likely to produce a stronger income stream, but their high liquidity makes them far easier to manage.

Assemble Your Dream Team
If you managed to get this far, your foundational knowledge on how to make money work for you already places you far in front of other people your age. But don't get too excited just yet because none of us is as smart as all of us. Even the most experienced investors seek expert guidance. Surrounding yourself with a team of trusted professionals including a clever accountant, a couple of creative brokers, a dozen realtors, and one or two trustworthy property managers can make a world of difference. They not only provide expert advice but also allow you to delegate tasks that are not your forte. It's like having a pit crew in a car race; you focus on driving while they make sure your vehicle is in top shape.

Let's be real; mastering financial concepts takes time, and you'll need all the help you can get. A good accountant will help you optimise your tax exposure, while a savvy broker could make all the difference between locking in the deal of the decade or losing tens or even hundreds of thousands in unearned profits due to lack of finance. So, once you're comfortable with the basics, start putting together your team. These are the people who will help you achieve your financial goals and create lasting wealth. Think of it as your personal guard, but for finance.

Be Conscious in Your Execution

Understanding the theory is one thing, but the rubber meets the road when you execute. Once you're ready to take that leap, proceed with caution. Be aware of confirmation and recency biases, especially as you gain experience, because that's when you're most vulnerable. Investing should never feel like a gamble. It should be a calculated move influenced by a conservative mindset, backed by extensive research, and in consultation with your team.

Think of your investments like a vegetable garden that's under your care. Water your crops regularly and keep a close eye on your cash flow. Cultivate the wondrous power of compounding, which can make a tiny seed grow into a towering tree, but be cautious with leverage, for it is like a potent fertiliser. If used wisely, it can supercharge your soil. But if you overuse it, it can ruin it. To ensure a bountiful harvest, you'll need to prune away underperforming assets before they become invasive weeds, while giving your star performers the space and nutrients they need to flourish. Distributing your resources appropriately is key.

Don't Stop Here: Keep Learning!

Benjamin Franklin once said that an investment in knowledge pays the best interest. Now imagine if you invested in learning about investing. That's what I call compounding returns! I've shared some book recommendations at the end to get you started.

Please, dear, keep in mind that what I've shared here is just a starting point. Developing your financial quotient will take far more than a handful of analogies from your old man. It is crucial that you educate yourself further and consult with trusted professionals before making any significant financial decisions.

Make Money Your Servant, Not Your Master

Money provides the means for crafting the life you desire, so don't treat it as the end goal. It is merely a tool. I cannot stress this enough. Understanding finance is crucial, but don't lose sight of what matters the most. Your health, your relationships, and your happiness can't be quantified in dollars and cents. Many people will tell you this, but pay close attention to how they say it, because anyone who speaks negatively about money or wealth will never have either and will resent you if you do.

Understanding the concept of money management and learning to implement the most tried and tested strategies for wealth creation will help you gain independence and give you the means to be kinder and more generous with your time, attention, and money.

The stoic philosopher Seneca once said, "It is not the man who has too little, but the man who craves more, that is poor." Remember that the goal is not just to accumulate wealth but to use it as a catalyst for a fulfilling life. Lack begets anxiety, greed, and misery, while abundance can foster joy, generosity, and contentment. Abundance is good. Always welcome it.

Baby, I want you to have enough. Enough to pursue your ambitions, enough to have freedom of choice, and enough to spread love and compassion. It's never too early to take control of your finances. Start today, make educated choices, and seize control of your future.

As you master the complexities of finance, however, don't lose sight of the fact that the most valuable investments you can ever make are in the people you love and in the good you can do in the world. And never forget, my darling, that the best things in life aren't things at all; they're moments and the people we share them with.

"A spouse is what you get when you marry your in-laws."
Alex Alvarez

Invest Well:
Choose Your Partner Wisely

Life presents us with a myriad of choices—what career to pursue, where to live, how to spend our time. But few decisions compare in gravity to choosing a spouse. This is the person who'll share your joys, your sorrows, your bank account, and quite possibly your genetic material for future generations. When you select a life partner, you're not just choosing someone you'll grow old with. You're selecting the co-author of your life story, your co-protagonist in every chapter from the moment you say, "I do."

The Most Important Choice of Your Life
Marriage is like a team sport where you're the manager, and choosing your spouse is like spending half the team's budget drafting a promising star player. You spend a fortune hoping that they will lead your team to the finals, but oftentimes, they flame out mid-season, your team gets demoted, and you get fired. Then, after the other teams learn what happened, you end up sidelined, with no one willing to give you another shot.

I don't say this lightly. Marriage is a lifelong commitment. It's being able to look at the other person and think, "Yes, I could spend a lifetime with you—making mistakes, fixing them, celebrating victories, learning from defeats, enduring hardships—and still love you just as much, if not more."

Now, let's not get too rosy either. Marriage is not a fairy tale where you ride off into the sunset, and that's the end. Far from it. It's a complex, ongoing narrative filled with unexpected twists, plot holes, and endless incongruencies. There's no two ways about it. You and your partner must be compatible. Your views on politics, debt, investment, retirement, or whether to have kids, pets or both, are not small matters. It is vital to discuss these topics openly, and early, to ensure that you're on the same page—or at the very least reading from the same book. That includes your in-laws too.

When your mother and I got our families together for the first time, my parents decided to have an embarrassing and rather pointless argument the instant your mother's parents came out to greet them. My mum was wearing high heels, expensive jewellery, and one to two kilos of makeup. My dad, in stark contrast, wore jeans, a polo shirt, and a silly flat brimmed baseball cap. After the dust settled, we went to a steakhouse where my mother thought it'd be appropriate to call everyone a hypocrite for pretending to be so civilised. She then ripped the leg of a roasted chicken with her bare hands and proceeded to eat it like a "non-hypocrite." To my astonishment, your mum's family burst in laughter and immediately joined the barehanded chicken club.

I must add that your mother's mum was overdressed too, and apart from the now infamous baseball cap responsible for my parents' earlier scuffle, your two grandpas were basically wearing the same outfit.

As you can see, socioeconomic differences, or as in this case, similarities, also matter greatly. If you can't imagine us and your partner's family going on holidays together or sitting through dinner at a restaurant without worrying about who'll go rogue with a fork—yep, been there—then that's a major red flag. Even if both your families give you space and stay out of your affairs as a couple—a naïve expectation, by the way—a significant wealth disparity between you and your partner is likely to create serious issues down the road.

Choosing the right partner can mean the difference between a story filled with love, support, and mutual growth, and one fraught with conflict, divergence, and resentment. Can you still recall the story of how your mother and I ended up in Australia? The uncertainty, the debates, the fear? It wasn't just about setting up a new home base; it was about building our future; your future. Our teamwork, our shared vision, and our trust in each other helped us get through our obstacles effectively, even when staying put and giving up on our dreams might have felt like the safest choice. These are the foundations of our successful relationship.

Your mum and I have always been a team. From the get-go, we've tackled every major decision as a unit. We decided to move in together, we migrated to different countries, and we even earned specific qualifications to meet tricky immigration criteria. But of all the decisions we made, the most meaningful was about when, where, and how to welcome you into our world. We didn't just wing it; we analysed our options and weighed the risks. And let me tell you, we had our share of arguments. I mean, how could we not? Life wasn't pitching us softballs; these were curveballs and they were painting all four corners. But you know what held us together? Unity, trust, a shared vision, and an unbreakable commitment to each other—and later, to you.

These are the pillars that have kept our home standing. They're the same pillars you'll need in all your relationships, whether they're friends, family, or your life partner. So guard these pillars well, and regularly check for cracks, because when life's storms come rumbling in—and they will—these pillars are what will keep your home standing too.

In the pages that follow, we'll delve into the nuts and bolts of what it means to choose a life partner. We'll discuss essential qualities to seek in a spouse, why it's crucial to align on values, and the importance of continuous effort from both sides.

Consider this your guide to making the most impactful decision that you will ever make. After all, your husband won't just be someone that you live with; he shall be someone that you simply cannot imagine your life without; the father of your children . . . and your mother's son-in-law.

When I Met Your Mother
We've all heard the clichés about love at first sight; about that mysterious spark that's supposed to change everything. While that might make for great romance novels or Hollywood endings, real life—and real love—is far more nuanced.

My experience with your mother was quite unique. I was incredibly lucky to have met her when I did. I was about to embark on an arduous immigration adventure where the last thing I needed was the distraction of a long streak of meaningless teenage girlfriends. Meeting your mother at 14 changed the game for me. Committing to her from the start freed me from riding the emotional rollercoaster of having to figure out relationships at an age when I had barely just started to get to know myself. Otherwise, I would've ended up with nothing but trauma, biases, and prejudices that could have ruined future relationships.

Meeting and choosing your mother at such a young age gave me the opportunity to connect with "the one and only," without bringing any relationship baggage into our lives.

In full disclosure, when I met your mother, I did feel that so-called spark go off, and at the time, I was convinced it was love. But now that I'm more mature and have enjoyed—and endured—20 years of marriage, I recognise that that spark was not love. It was just a chemical reaction compelling me to pair with someone I recognised as a suitable mate. That's all. Falling in love is intense, it's real, but it doesn't last. And that's ok. Being perpetually in love may sound beautiful in theory, but in practice, spending one's emotional resources at such rate, day in and day out, could only end in disaster. Such strong emotions aren't meant to last so long. It's not only unhealthy, but impractical.

True love is to no longer think of your partner as someone you're in love with, but as a part of you. For example, I like my nose. I can't imagine my life without it. I need it to breathe, to smell a nice meal, and to enjoy your scent when we cuddle. But I'm not "in love" with my nose. Yet, I would never be tempted to cut it off simply because I came across another nose that looked more appealing. Sounds absurd, doesn't it? That's my point. When you're in love, you don't think this way. You only learn to think this way when you genuinely and wholeheartedly learn to love someone. And that's something you can only experience after fully committing to a lifetime together.

As my long-distance relationship with your mother unfolded, we talked . . . a lot. We shared our values, our aspirations, our fears, and our interpretation of what a fulfilling life would look like. We discussed politics, religion, marriage, children, and our relationship with money—a subject I kept bringing up in our conversations.

We talked about our families, our friends, and why those relationships mattered to us. In essence, we got to know each other, for real. After nearly two years of this, she moved in with me. And guess what? We did not have a whirlwind romance because we were no longer in love. What we had was better—a deep friendship, mutual respect, aligned ambitions, and the aspiration to grow old together. We both had our flaws, but it was the joy in accepting each other's imperfections that made us realise we had something special, something that could last . . . something that did last.

To wed someone is far more than signing a marriage contract. It's a covenant—a solemn, heartfelt commitment to work together through whatever comes your way, especially when the road gets tough. Finding the right spouse isn't about ticking boxes or fitting someone into your ideal mould. It's about how you evolve together, how you team up to face life's challenges, and how you both contribute to each other's growth and fulfillment. Your husband should not just be a witness to your life; he must be an active participant, a co-conspirator in your shared life story—your partner for life. And the same goes for you.

Social Circles: The Hidden Influence

When it comes to relationships, we often hear the term "opposites attract." While that might be true in some cases, it's crucial to remember that attraction is fleeting. And when you choose to marry someone, you're not just marrying them—you're entering into a contract with their entire social circle. Friends, family, colleagues, and yes, exes too—they all become a part of your life, directly or indirectly.

I've known men and women who ignored this crucial aspect, focusing solely on their partner without considering the broader picture. Many ended up feeling isolated or torn between their spouse and a social circle they could never fully engage with or even trust. A supportive network of relationships outside the marital bond is conducive to a strong, lasting marriage.

I didn't just like your mother; I genuinely liked her family too. How could I not? It was her cousin that introduced us. They were decent people who shared our values and life perspectives, and they're now my family too, reinforcing our marriage's strength. And let's face it, in marriage, you'll need all the help you can get. You want a partner whose support network complements and enriches your own.

As we discussed earlier, you become the average of the people you spend the most time with. This principle is magnified tenfold when you are in a romantic relationship. If your boyfriend's circle lifts you both up, that's a net gain that increases your chances of long-term success as a couple. But if you find yourself constantly at odds with his social circle, that's a big enough red flag to reconsider your future together.

So, when you're choosing a spouse, look around and pay attention. Who are they surrounded by? What values do those people hold? And most importantly, could you see them becoming a part of your life in a meaningful way? A marriage isn't an isolated entity; it's part of a broader network of social connections and relationships. Make sure it's a network you'd be proud to be a part of.

Shared Values: The Foundation of a Strong Partnership
Choosing a spouse is a monumental decision; one that must not be about love or compatibility on the surface. What fortifies a relationship for the long haul is shared values. Values are the deeply ingrained principles that guide your actions; they're the

"why" behind what you do. So it's imperative that your lifelong partner aligns with you in this way.

I've witnessed too many good people marry for love, only to find out down the track that they wanted fundamentally different things in life. Whether it was how they envisioned raising a family, their career ambitions, or their views on money, these mismatches created a chasm that love alone was unable to bridge.

Your mother and I shared key values that have been the bedrock of our relationship. We both value family above all else, which is why I'm writing this book for you, my love. I won't deny this, though. We've picked up a few scars in our journey together. But our common values have helped us navigate life's highs and lows without getting lost along the way.

Now, I'm not saying that you and your partner should be carbon copies of each other; individuality has its own merit. Besides, you won't agree on everything. No couple does. But your core values must align, because when times get tough, these are the principles you'll fall back on. They are the framework within which your lives will be constructed, so they'd better be sturdy, and they'd better fit well.

At the core, you should share the same ethical and moral compass. When this condition is met, the choices you make in life will naturally align, saving you from countless arguments and heartache. To quote Nietzsche, "Marriage is a long conversation." If you want that conversation to be fruitful, it must be grounded on these principles.

Common Goals: Your North Star
If love is the fuel that starts a relationship, and shared values form the engine that keeps it going, then common goals are the

navigation system that tells you where you're going. Imagine embarking on a journey with your husband, holding hands and eager for the adventure. But then, you find that your compasses point in different directions. It's not long before you're lost in a maze of conflicting priorities, stress, and disillusionment.

Your mother and I always discussed our goals in life—not just in passing but with intention. We spoke about growing old together, how we envisioned ourselves as parents, and the kind of legacy we hoped to leave behind. These discussions served as our North Star, guiding us through life and keeping us aligned even through the thickest fog.

Common goals help you make decisions that are coherent and beneficial for both of you. Whether they are financial, familial, or personal, they become achievable when you're both pulling in the same direction. It's like rowing a canoe; if you're not in sync, you'll either go in circles or end up tipped over.

Antoine de Saint-Exupéry, author of The Little Prince, said that love does not consist in gazing at each other, but in looking outward together in the same direction. This is a simple yet profound reminder that love isn't just about the present moment but about building a future together.

Communication: More Than Words
In a relationship, words are the building blocks and silence is the gaps in between. Just like the foundation of a house, both are necessary, but if either one is off, you risk the whole structure collapsing. So, if you're contemplating marrying someone, make sure your communication foundation is rock-solid.

We often associate communication with words, but in practice, it's more about understanding and being understood.

This encompasses everything from simple day-to-day banter to navigating complex emotional issues. If you can't communicate effectively with your partner, even the most straightforward decisions can become a minefield.

Throughout this cancer ordeal, your mother and I have shared moments when words have failed us, overwhelmed by the sheer gravity of what we were facing. But even in those moments when words weren't enough, our years together enabled us to understand each other's silence, each other's fears, and each other's love.

To find someone you can authentically communicate with is to discover a symbiosis of the heart and the mind. Yes, you'll have disagreements, but hopefully they'll simply become opportunities for growth instead of catalysts for resentment. A relationship that can't survive disagreements is like a ship that can't weather a storm—it's only a matter of time before it sinks.

One of the best pieces of advice I can offer you, darling, comes from James Baldwin: "You think your pain and your heartbreak are unprecedented in the history of the world, but then you read." The point is that effective communication involves a combination of empathy, openness, and the wisdom to know that your experiences are part of a greater human story.

A Lifelong Commitment

Love can be intoxicating, but it's not the end-all, be-all. In choosing a life partner, you're also choosing a lifestyle, a family, and very likely, a set of challenges that could either elevate you or bring you down. Saying "I do" is akin to tying your shoelaces before a marathon—you're making a commitment to stick it out, even when you're parched and your legs are about to give out.

Marriage is a lifelong commitment complete with its own set of highs, lows, and periods of monotony. That means having the patience and the resilience to work through issues together. You will inevitably experience periods in your marriage when love is on the backburner, overshadowed by mundane routines and the common stressors of life. But it's in those very periods that your commitment to each other is tested and fortified.

My advice to you, my darling, is to envision the person you hold dear during good times and bad times. Is he cheering for you when you're basking in glory? More importantly, is he holding your hand when you're facing your hardest trials? These questions can guide you in selecting a husband who becomes not just your "better than nothing" companion, but your true partner for life.

Like your mum and I, you and your husband will have your own unique set of challenges. But having the mindset that marriage is forever will help you tackle them together. As Nietzsche put it, "It is not a lack of love, but a lack of friendship that makes unhappy marriages." Marriage, more than a contract to share resources, is a pact to be best friends, even when you're at odds with each other.

In the United States, nearly 50% of marriages end in divorce. The situation isn't much better in Australia, where 30% of first-time marriages and a staggering 60% of subsequent marriages meet the same fate. Those are not good odds. Contrast that with India, where over 90% of marriages are arranged and the divorce rate barely cracks 1%. It makes you wonder, doesn't it? The reason for this may lie in some consumer psychology I studied back in business school. The research showed that when people are presented with either a multitude of choices or the option to "return" their purchase, that they often end up less satisfied. In other words, fewer choices and a "no returns" policy seem to lead to greater contentment. So, it's not all that surprising that arranged marriages, which generally offer fewer choices and discourage divorce, tend to be more enduring.

When calling it quits is frowned upon by society, married couples become more successful at solving their issues because they're committed to staying together. Having endless choices and society's seal of approval to end your marriage on a whim may seem empowering, but it's more likely a hindrance preventing couples in individualist societies from committing to each other wholeheartedly.

In a society where nearly half of the adult population treats marriage as if it were a returnable product purchased from a department store, a different approach is crucial. Entering a marriage as an unbreakable bond will set you up for finding the right partner and building a life together underpinned by the love, support, understanding, and companionship that you'll both deserve.

The point here is not to say you must never break up—let's be real; sometimes it's necessary. The point is to do everything you can to choose the right partner before you get married so that you don't have to. Once all the cards are dealt, and you and your partner are equally convinced that you've found each other's one-and-only for better or for worse, for richer or for poorer, in sickness and in health, to love and to cherish, until death do you part, then you're ready. And later in life—but sooner than you think—when you enter that stage when fairy tale love takes a backseat, don't let your judgement be clouded by what will seem like an endless buffet of romantic options. Your commitment to each other is what will lead to the kind of love I'm talking about; the kind that's real.

One Last Thing
Baby, I haven't dictated your choices—whether about your career path, or your hair and makeup (that's your mum's department). But one thing I will ask: I implore you to steer clear of those hookup apps designed to "efficiently" pair people up. Humans are not products to be picked out of a catalogue, and your lifelong partner is unlikely to be found in one. I'm not saying that it's impossible to find love this way, but finding love and finding your lifelong partner are different goals. The odds of the latter are not in your favour when using these services.

You'll have a far better chance of meeting the man of your life if you start within your own circle—after all, you've chosen those people for a reason. Your mum and I met through one of her cousins, one of your aunties who has always been dear to me. From that point forward, dating was off the table. Through thick and thin, your mother and I have faced every challenge life could throw at us, and still, we managed to prevail.

In the 25 years we've been together, we've seen too many loving marriages fail, leaving too many innocent children torn between broken households. It's tragic. So understand this and understand it well: Love doesn't keep a marriage going; commitment does.

Like any couple, your mum and I have had our share of disagreements. Yet, our commitment to our marriage and our love for you have always been the cornerstones of our relationship. This has lifted our union above any fleeting differences or selfish wants we may have had along the way. Even without you in the picture, the idea of life apart never made sense for us. We grew up together, evolved together, and in doing so, became a singular unit.

To me, this might be the greatest success story ever told, but no hookup app would consider our story a success because their business model thrives on singles staying single. Think about it: if you ever found "the one," then you'd no longer be a paying customer. So choose your partner wisely, and always remember that you're not just choosing for yourself; you're choosing for your future children too.

"Your network is your net worth."
Porter Gale

Find Your Family: Bond with Purpose

Family isn't just a group of blood relatives. It can also extend to the organisations and communities that you associate yourself with, and these bonds matter a great deal. Some families you are born into, some you marry into, others you graduate into, and others you join for a fee.

Your values act as your internal GPS, guiding your actions and decisions through the labyrinth of life. Imagine trying to complete a complex puzzle but ignoring the picture on the box. You'd be left fitting random pieces together, hoping for a coherent outcome. That's what life's like when your actions aren't aligned with your values. Now, extend that logic to relationships. It stands to reason that the people you bring into your social circle should resonate with your core beliefs and principles.

Would you feel comfortable taking career advice from someone who doesn't value discipline, integrity, or hard work? I hope not. Similarly, aligning your friendships and associations with your own personal and professional values adds a layer of richness and depth to those relationships. Not only will these relationships feel more satisfying, but they'll also serve as a source of consistent support and encouragement, helping you live a life that's true to who you are.

Reciprocity: The Two-Way Street of Relationships

It takes two to tango. Relationships can be a beautiful dance of give-and-take if you let them. Consider it a form of social karma; what you put in often comes back to you in unexpected and rewarding ways. Networking isn't a solo endeavour—it's a communal activity that's built on mutual benefits. If you enter a relationship thinking only about what you can extract from it, you're missing half the picture. There's a deep sense of satisfaction that comes from helping someone else, from making someone's day a bit better because you are in it.

Think of your relationships as two-way streets, not one-way lanes that only lead to you. Offer your wisdom, share your resources, and lend a helping hand when able. When you put positive energy out there, you're not just doing someone else a favour; you're also enriching your own experience. The beauty of this reciprocity is that it creates a ripple effect in the fabric of your existence. Your actions, however small, can cause a cascade of kindness, enriching not only your own experience but your community's as well.

Diversity: A Symphony of Perspectives

The world's a big place, filled with people from all walks of life. Your neighbourhood, your workplace, your social circles — they're all microcosms of the world at large. Instituting diversity in your network isn't just a trendy talking point for business circles; it's a critical strategy for personal and professional growth.

People from different backgrounds, industries, and life experiences bring a richness to your life that can't be measured. They challenge your views, introduce you to new perspectives, and expand your frame of reference.

Would you only read books from one section of the library? Of course not. Life is no different. Why limit yourself to one type of connection? A well-rounded network isn't just a privilege; it's an asset.

Unlocking Possibilities: A Top MBA
Here's a target that may not be on your radar yet, but one you should pin on your kanban board, for it will have a significant impact on your life—completing an MBA from a top business school. It's not just an investment in education; it's an investment in yourself. It's also not about learning how to crunch numbers or how to develop business strategies—although both are sufficiently helpful to make it worth your while. The true value of a top MBA lies in the "family" you join, the network you enter, and the broadened perspectives you'll gain from peers who, like you, aim to excel.

Going to a top business school is akin to joining an elite club. The connections made there can last a lifetime and open doors you never even knew existed.

Why a top business school? What's wrong with the more affordable MBA program offered at your local university or business institute? Because top business schools attract the best of the best from all over the world. These are the high achievers, the innovative thinkers, the ambitious professionals who will eventually lead in their chosen fields. But more importantly, it's the group of people who will form your support system—one that extends far beyond the classroom.

However, completing a top MBA is only beneficial if you go in with an open mind, because only then, will you be ready to absorb what this unique "family" has to offer without getting held back by cynicism and bias.

Network Investing: The Compounding Interest of Relationships
Since we've already covered the magic of compound interest in the world of finance, I would like to introduce you now to its social equivalent—networking. Creating a network is not just about short-term gains; it's a long-term investment in your personal and professional development. And like any good investment, the benefits may not be immediate, but they tend to grow exponentially over time.

Think of it this way: Every relationship you nurture adds another layer of strength to your support system. Given enough time, these layers compound, providing a wealth of emotional and professional resources that you can tap into as needed. But this only happens if you're in it for the long run, nurturing these connections year after year, much like a skilled chef perfects a recipe through constant refinement and attention to detail.

The Real Deal
We've all been in that awkward spot, haven't we? Putting on a persona, toning down our quirks, or even amplifying them to fit into a particular group or environment. But here's the kicker: people can generally sniff out inauthenticity from a mile away, so it's not a scent you want to be wearing. While it's often wise to ease into new environments and situations with a slightly more "vanilla" version of who you are until you've gotten a good read of the room, don't let this come at the expense of your

essence. As Ralph Waldo Emerson put it, "To be yourself in a world that is constantly trying to make you something else is the greatest accomplishment."

Being authentic doesn't mean you must lay all your cards on the table right from the get-go. It's more about maintaining a level of openness and realness that allows for trust to be built progressively. You don't have to spill your deepest secrets to prove you're genuine. Instead, let your actions speak for themselves. This isn't hypocritical. This is what we call "poise." Trust is the cornerstone of any relationship, and nothing builds trust faster than being your true self. You'll find that the relationships built on authenticity are the ones that endure through the ages.

Your Personal Board of Directors
Lastly, let's talk about your inner circle, the key players of your network, your starting line-up. Think of this group as your personal board of directors—the folks you turn to when you need advice, emotional support, or a fresh perspective. Unlike a sprawling network of acquaintances, this is a compact, effective team of individuals whose opinions you hold in high regard.

Invest deeply in these relationships. Like fine wine, they get better with time when kept in the right conditions. Nourish these bonds, show up for these individuals, and give them opportunities to show up for you. You'll encounter all sorts of people along your journey, but it's those you let into this inner circle that make the most meaningful impact on your life. They're not just friends or mentors; they're your chosen family.

To sum up, starting a family isn't just about getting married and having children. It's about choosing your tribe, associating with others deliberately, and bonding intentionally with clarity and purpose. The music you listen to, the sports teams you cheer for, the social causes you support, and your alma matter, are all families. Each should serve a purpose, because these are the networks that sustain you, not just emotionally, but intellectually and professionally as well, so be mindful of your associations.

Choose your family with care and intention, and never forget that the true power of your network lies primarily in the depth of its connections, not just in its breadth.

"The stock market is filled with individuals who know the price of everything, but the value of nothing."
Philip Fisher

Plan Beyond: Nurture Your Nest

Money can be a double-edged sword. On one side, it offers freedom, opportunities, and a sense of security. On the other, it evokes stress, envy, and even a sense of emptiness when it's misunderstood or mismanaged. But money isn't inherently evil, nor is it the epitome of happiness. What matters is your relationship with it, how you earn it, how you manage it, and most importantly, how you use it to create a meaningful life.

Our goal should not be to amass an obscene amount of wealth just for the sake of it. There's no shortage of seemingly successful people who are slaves to their riches—always checking stock prices, fretting over real estate market fluctuations, always obsessed with amassing more. These individuals often miss the point; they understand the price of everything but the value of nothing. So, it's important to be sensible about this. I want you to find a balance. Be savvy with your finances but be mindful that the numbers in your bank account aren't the end game; they are merely an indicator of one aspect of your existence.

Building wealth means different things to different people. For your mother, it meant creating a comfortable life for you, ensuring you had access to good education, and leaving enough behind for you to take forward. For me, it meant all those things too, but at first, it was all about safety; first for all of us, then for just you and your mother. But once those bricks were laid, I set my sights on the next milestone: generational wealth.

I want you to think of money as a tool, a resource you can use to construct your life. It's like the cement in a building; without it, your plans might crumble, but an overabundance can make the structure rigid and lifeless. Knowing how much is enough will give you the freedom to live your life on your terms—whether that means taking a year off to travel, investing in a cause that's close to your heart, or starting your own business with the confidence and the peace of mind of knowing that you have permission, and the means, to start over fresh if things don't work out.

Keep in mind that the wealthier you become, the larger the nest you can build and the greater the number of eggs you can take under your wing. It's not just about supporting your immediate family but also about creating opportunities for others, helping your community, and ideally building something that will last long beyond your lifetime.

Why Bother?
Baby, let's get one thing straight—making money isn't a bad thing, nor is wanting to accumulate wealth. The point is to understand what we're amassing it for. You'll find that people often chase after riches as if they were chasing a setting sun, thinking they can capture it and hold it forever. But the reality is, the sun sets whether we want it to or not, and a new day dawns. Wealth works much the same way.

You've probably heard that money can't buy happiness, but that's only partially true. Money buys options, opportunities, and many degrees of freedom. It allows us to chase dreams that would otherwise be out of reach, and it gives us the power to effect positive change — not just in our own lives but in the lives of others.

Imagine that at last, you found the proverbial pot of gold. It would be tempting to just hoard it, to keep it all for yourself. That's an instinct we all have. But if you look a bit beyond, you'll see that you have the power to extend the benefits of that gold to others — maybe set up a scholarship, fund a school in a developing country, or support medical research that could save lives. This isn't about being a hero; it's about acknowledging the broader responsibility that comes with abundance.

You don't need to be a billionaire to make a difference; even small or non-financial contributions can create a ripple effect. Helping a friend get a job, organising your community to purchase from a small family business recovering from a fire, hosting a newly arrived international student until they can secure their own place — these are all interventions that can have a profoundly positive effect in the lives of those impacted. Even we have been the beneficiaries of a generous amount of charity and goodwill. Our last Christmas dinner and the toys you received, personal loans from family, the fundraiser that my business school mates held to help us hold the fort this last year; all of that has had a profound effect on our lives since my diagnosis. It is now my mission to get well, jump back on the horse, and begin paying it forward.

I want you to grasp this: wealth isn't just about personal comfort and security. It's a tool you can use to carve out a better world for everyone, including future generations. When used wisely, it amplifies your capacity for good. And in the end, my love, true wealth is not measured by what we accumulate but by what we can afford to give away.

Generational Wealth: Laying the Groundwork
One of the most compelling aspects of building wealth is the possibility of setting up not just your immediate family, but your children's as well. That's what your mother and I have been working our whole lives to achieve.

In addition to your own earnings and endeavours, the financial groundwork we lay while you're still little can become a launching pad for you to soar even higher. But it's more than just setting aside money for your education or your first home. What we're aiming for transcends mere financial savings; it's about laying a foundation that you and your future generations can build upon.

Remember, the nest you build does not only need to house your own eggs; it's a legacy that can offer warmth, nourishment, security, and opportunity to others as well.

You see, generational wealth isn't just about passing on assets; it's about passing on a mindset. It's teaching you to fish rather than just giving you a fish. By instilling values around becoming self-sufficient, financially savvy, and generous, I hope to pass on a legacy of not just wealth, but wisdom. Imagine knowing that you've not just lived a good life but set the stage for your children, their children, and beyond. That's true wealth.

Nevertheless, building generational wealth isn't just about making money; it's also about keeping it. You'll encounter numerous temptations to spend on goods you don't need, to invest recklessly, or even to lend money without due diligence. Resist these urges.

The idea isn't to turn you into a miser but to inculcate the importance of thoughtful spending and investment. It's about making choices today that future generations will thank you for.

The old saying, "shirtsleeves to shirtsleeves in three generations" describes the tendency for wealth to be lost by the third generation. The first generation works hard to build wealth from scratch, often starting with nothing (like your grandparents). The second generation maintains or even grows the wealth, usually because they've witnessed firsthand the effort that went into building it (like your mother and me). And the third generation, having grown up in affluence but without the experience of working for it, is often less mindful or appreciative of the value of money. As a result, they may squander the wealth, sinking the family right back to where they started—please, don't let this be you. I've worked my entire life for our family to buck this trend, not for the sake of hoarding wealth, but to continue the good that can be done with it. Just as your mother and I are building a nest for you, I want you to be able to do the same for your children and theirs.

Money: A Force for Good

Darling, the wealth you accumulate does more than just secure your future. It acts as a catalyst for change, a resource that can be channelled to amplify the impact you have on the world around you. When you're financially secure, you have the freedom to make choices unbounded by urgency or need. You can take the time to identify where your resources would serve the highest purpose. This is where the true power of wealth lies.

Think of philanthropy not as an obligation but as an opportunity. For instance, leaving politics aside, the billionaires of my time, through their foundations, have invested billions in healthcare, education, and poverty alleviation. Now, I'm not saying you need to be a magnate to make a difference. As we covered earlier, even small contributions to causes close to your heart can set ripples in motion that may turn into waves of change. Unfortunately, large charitable organisations often allocate a significant portion of their budget to administrative costs. Therefore, direct contributions to those in need usually make the most impact, creating ripples that last longer. And if you have the option to donate food, clothing or money, always donate money. Money gives people and small charities the agency to spend it on what they truly need, as opposed to what you might assume they need due to personal biases or, as is often the case, due to poor marketing.

But it's not just about donating money; you can leverage your financial standing to influence change directly. Perhaps you'll find an innovative solution to a societal issue and have the financial backing to bring it to life. Or maybe, you'll sponsor a scholarship, giving opportunities to a deserving student who might otherwise go overlooked. You don't have to register a charity or make this complicated. In the case of a scholarship, contact the school of your choice, choose a student, and pay their tuition. It's that simple. You might even consider mentoring them if they're interested. That's the beauty of wealth; it gives you options.

Through these avenues, you're not just spending money; you're investing in a better world. As you've probably gathered, money amplifies who you are and what you care about. If you're compassionate, it allows you to express that compassion in a grander way. If you believe in justice, it gives you the resources to make things right. Money, in the hands of good people, can do extraordinary things.

Generational Wealth: The Legacy of a Lifetime

Generational wealth is not just about passing down assets, though that's a significant part of it. It's also about imparting wisdom, ethics, a sense of justice, and a philanthropic spirit. While estate planning, trusts, and wills are essential, what's equally crucial is imparting the values that made it possible to accumulate and manage that wealth in the first place.

Imagine, my darling, a future where you, your children, and their children aren't bound by financial need. A future where your family can focus on contributions, on making the world a better place. This is what I mean by planning beyond. It's not just planning for your retirement or for a rainy day; it's laying the foundation for a legacy that could extend far beyond your lifetime.

It's a comforting thought to know that your children won't have to start from scratch, that they'll have a leg up in a world that often seems more interested in placing hurdles along the track than in helping you run the race. They'll start their adult lives not in a ditch but on a runway, primed for takeoff. Such shall be their privilege. And this, baby, is one of the greatest gifts a parent can offer: the freedom of choice.

As you navigate life's complexities, remember that the ultimate measure of our success lies in the experiences we accumulate, the love we share, and the lives we uplift. The well-placed bricks of generational wealth, built with both financial responsibility and a moral compass, will be the foundation for generations of changemakers — compassionate, innovative, and endowed with the freedom to choose their path. And this, my love, is the legacy I leave you — a torch for you to carry forward, ever bright, and ever enduring.

"You have two lives, and the second begins when you realise you only have one."
Seneca

Embrace Your Mortality: Live Well, Leave a Legacy

From the instant we're born, we're on a countdown. It's a sobering truth. Some of us will reach the end sooner than others, but the destination is the same for all. Still, particularly when we're young, we tend to act as though we've got endless time, as if the rules of mortality apply only to others or, as you used to think until recently, to those who turn 100 years old. Life, however, has a way of snapping us back to reality—often through illness or unexpected loss. It jolts us awake for a moment, but then, as routine sets back in, that awareness fades . . . and we forget.

Leave Well
You'll often hear that life is short, but as the stoic Seneca posited, it's not that life is inherently short, but that we waste much of it. Nothing could have reflected this profound truth more so than when I saw my reflection in the bathroom mirror the morning after my diagnosis. I thought to myself, "This is it. From now on, for the rest of my life, the rest of my life will never mean the same." Paradoxically, I also felt a strange sense of relief when I reached the realisation that . . . I lived well.

Think about the common expressions we use to describe life's transience: "Time flies," "It happened in the blink of an eye," or "Before you know it." We say these phrases often but rarely grasp the full weight of their meaning. In the grand scheme of things, our lives are but mere moments — fleeting, fragile and precious. Every second that ticks away is a second that you'll never get back. Yet, acknowledging this can be liberating and life changing. Knowing that your life is finite can imbue the mere act of waking up in the morning with the weight and importance it deserves.

This is not a call to drop everything and run off to some distant island, leaving all responsibilities behind — although, if that aligns with your values, I won't stop you. It's a call to live deliberately, to avoid squandering your limited time by cruising on autopilot. Whether you're buried in textbooks, grinding through a workday, or watching a sunset, try to be present, because in each of these moments lies a lifetime of experience, and each second is a universe of possibility just waiting to be explored.

For centuries, the notion of "living well" has captivated human imagination. Philosophers, poets, and even ordinary people like us have pondered its meaning. While interpretations may differ, one constant remains: quality trumps quantity. A short life lived well holds infinitely more value than a long life merely endured. I'm not advocating that you adopt a hedonistic lifestyle; rather, I'm emphasising the importance of understanding the impact of every decision you make, every relationship you nurture, and every moment you savour.

Imagine coming to the end of your days, flipping through the proverbial photo album of your life. What would you like to see? Pages filled with smiles, loving memories and rich experiences or empty slots where pictures should have been—pictures that you were too busy, too scared, or too cautious to take. As the saying goes, life is not measured by the number of breaths we take, but by the moments that take our breath away.

I want you to look at your life as an evolving mural rather than a fixed, unchangeable canvas. Mistakes will happen; they're the smudges and accidental brushstrokes that contribute to your masterpiece. Treat them as tuition fees for life's most poignant lessons. Pay them and move on. A life well lived is about fully absorbing each experience, emotion, and interaction. And if you can, do so as if it were your last—because one day, it will be.

Some of the most damaging words you'll ever hear are, "Don't worry, you've got time." Never heed this advice, and don't let the knowledge that the clock is ticking merely linger in the back of your mind. Have the courage to bring it to the front. But tread carefully, as this reality could paralyse you, steering you towards a lifestyle focused more on avoiding risks than on seizing opportunities to live fully. A better choice would be to let this awareness empower you, serving as a continuous reminder that each new day is a precious gift, a rare opportunity to be unwrapped with enthusiasm and gratitude.

There's no simple answer to what it means to live well, but here's a starting point: Take time to reflect, to understand your core values and what gives your life meaning. Once you identify what genuinely matters to you, align your life with those principles. Suddenly, change seem less daunting, decisions become easier, and risks morph into opportunities. And don't just go through the motions—relish the journey. Laugh, love, and pour your heart into everything you do, because you've got only one shot at this. Make it count.

Leave a Legacy

My dear Alexandra, by now, I suppose you'll have read about how I became a citizen of the world. If you haven't, I might just have to haunt your mum until you crack open those pages. In short, it was an arduous, but overall positive journey. I travelled across borders, broke all kinds of barriers, and connected with people from all walks of life to learn the lessons that ultimately turned me into the man that became your father.

By embracing differences, tearing down walls, and finding common ground, I've built bridges across cultures, and the wisdom gained is what fills these pages to serve as your guide, so you don't have to navigate life's challenges as blindly as I did. But you don't have to follow my footsteps. If I've done my job right, you should have the resources to tread your own path and write your own story.

I have made it my life's mission to document my journey and my mistakes so you can have the freedom to make your own. All of this, sweetheart, I've done for you. I started in my mid-twenties because I had this nagging feeling that living a long life was not in the cards for me. So, I decided to document and publish my chronicles so that one day, when your mother had you with another loving husband, you would still get to know me; the man who would have become your father if his clock had only kept ticking.

Fortunately, life gave me the extension I needed to leave this world without regrets and with my heart filled to the brim with your love. But here I am again, facing the inevitable and unable to influence the outcome. Fate will decide if I'll ever get to read you these words, but should my time come before you grow up, I want you to know that it's ok. I'm ready. I travelled the hard road so that I could still be here with you today, if only on these pages, and safely carry you on my shoulders as you find your own way. So, don't be afraid, my dear. You will be fine. I spent my whole existence making sure of it.

My relentless perseverance throughout life was fuelled by my unyielding responsibility to create a stable and prosperous environment for you. My road was filled with challenges, sweat, and tears, but you were always at the core of my pursuits. It was not about becoming "successful" — whatever that means these days. It was about finding peace and security, for you. The long nights working and studying, my fastidious accounting efforts, my unabated dedication to everything I did, the crushing weight I always carried on my shoulders. It was not for me or my pointless career. It was about attaining and growing the resources that would one day give you the safety and the security to make your own choices in life, the choices I didn't get to make. It was about giving you a childhood defined by laughter and love, not by scarcity and fear.

Fulfillment is not a destination, sweetheart; it's an integral part of the journey itself. Remember when we built your LEGO city? Sitting on my lap while we played computer games? Visiting playgrounds and museums? Our many lunch dates? They were all part of a larger goal, the most important of them all: a life well lived.

I write these final words with a heavy heart, but one that is full of love, full of gratitude and, ironically, full of hope. These stories, these lessons, this wisdom ... they are a testament to our shared journey, to our dreams, to our love. Hold them close, for they are part of who we are as a family and who you are as an individual. Nevertheless, I want you to know that this book, the legacy I leave behind, is not my best work. That title belongs to you — you are my legacy, my greatest contribution to this world.

I trust you'll carry forth the love, the strength, and the wisdom to define and pursue your own destiny, and that you'll embrace the learning, the laughter, and even the tears, for I can't ask you to not cry for me when I'm gone. Instead, I ask you to reach into your heart to find me again, because, baby, I've never left you. I'm right here, loving you, believing in you, and cheering you on.

Yours forever,

Dad.

Recommended Reading

The following works present a rich mix of ideas, metaphors, arguments, and sometimes even instructions on how to comprehend the world and your place in it. Their messages will equip you with a sharper lens to decode the complexities of society and will also help you craft your own unique framework of understanding. Once you digest what these gifted authors have shared, your newfound perspective will further empower you to adeptly manoeuvre through an illogical world brimming with ambiguity, unspoken norms and unwritten rules. Enjoy the ride!

Philosophy
- ✓ On the Shortness of Life, by Seneca
- ✓ The Art of Living, by Epictetus
- ✓ The Art of Worldly Wisdom, by Baltasar Gracián
- ✓ 12 Rules for Life, by Jordan Peterson

Personal Development
- ✓ The Joys of Compounding: The Passionate Pursuit of Lifelong Learning, by Gautam Baid
- ✓ Man's Search for Meaning, by Viktor Frankl
- ✓ Atomic Habits, by James Clear
- ✓ Black Box Thinking, by Matthew Syed
- ✓ The Courage to Be Disliked, by I. Kishimi & F. Koga

Leadership
- ✓ Influence is Your Superpower: How to Get What You Want Without Compromising Who You Are, by Zoe Chance
- ✓ How to Win Friends and Influence People, by Dale Carnegie
- ✓ The Infinite Game, by Simon Sinek
- ✓ The Essential Drucker, by Peter Drucker
- ✓ The Prince, by Niccolo Machiavelli
- ✓ The 48 Laws of Power, by Robert Greene

Economics
- ✓ Basic Economics, by Thomas Sowell
- ✓ Freakonomics, by Steven Levitt and Stephen Dubner

Finance
- ✓ The Richest Man in Babylon, by George Clason
- ✓ Rich Dad, Poor Dad, by Robert T. Kiyosaki
- ✓ The Millionaire Next Door, by T. Stanley & W. Danko
- ✓ The Barefoot Investor, by Scott Pape

Learning & Education
- ✓ The Art of Thinking Clearly, by Rolf Dobelli
- ✓ Deep Work, by Cal Newport
- ✓ Outliers, by Malcom Gladwell
- ✓ On Education, by Bertrand Russell

Society & Justice
- ✓ The Vision of the Anointed, by Thomas Sowell
- ✓ The Trial, by Franz Kafka
- ✓ The Idiot, by Fyodor Dostoyevsky
- ✓ Nineteen Eighty-Four, by George Orwell
- ✓ Candide, by Voltaire

History
- ✓ Guns, Germs and Steel, by Jared Diamond
- ✓ Conquer or Die, by Ben Hughes

Health & Fitness
- ✓ Why We Sleep, by Matthew Walker
- ✓ Why We Get Fat, by Gary Taubes

Chronicles of a Nomad: Memoirs of an Immigrant

Sharing an insider's perspective on how many young migrants overcome their limitations to shape their own destinies, *Chronicles of a Nomad: Memoirs of an Immigrant*, is an introspective journey where a young man, the intrepid Carlos Rodriguez, bares his soul within the pages of his intimate memoirs.

Despite a privileged upbringing, fate thrusts him into the heart of socioeconomic turmoil in his once opulent homeland, so that at the tender age of fifteen, seeking safety, he emigrates to the United States, where he defies the odds and surrenders to the clutches of an expired tourist visa. Then, just as his path straightens, an unforeseen twist sends him on yet another expedition, this time to Greece, where he confronts the conundrum of seeking solace on foreign soil, even further removed from what he once knew as "home."

This cross-cultural adventure will lead you through three seemingly disparate countries, immersing you in a multitude of situations that balance humour and solemnity with a narration that brings together lessons learned about family, education, culture, religion, economy, politics, love, marriage and, of course, immigration.

While this novel is a work of fiction, it is inspired by the author's own journey and his encounters with fellow migrants along his path. Thus, it presents a captivating story defined by personal growth, culture shock, and the quest for self-discovery.

ISBN: 9789609309189

V2036: A Venezuelan Chronicle

Set against the backdrop of presidential elections, military uprisings, and international conflicts, Alex Alvarez's political thriller, *V2036: A Venezuelan Chronicle,* draws inspiration from Venezuela's tumultuous journey towards 21st Century Socialism.

A sequel to *Chronicles of a Nomad: Memoirs of an Immigrant,* this novel features a military ruler, an opposition activist, and an expatriated citizen in the roles that ultimately determine the fate of their nation. Will they guide Venezuela towards a brighter future or further plunge it into irreversible decline?

Pushing the boundaries of historical fiction, V2036 weaves a compelling narrative around pivotal moments in Venezuela's recent history, including the notable military uprisings of February 4 and November 27, 1991, as well as the civilian uprising of April 11, 2002. As the paths of the new protagonists intertwine, representing the most influential sectors of Venezuelan society, their audacious endeavours shed light on the complex challenges facing the Bolivarian Republic.

Join Carlos Rodríguez once again, this time as he reunites with his friend Bernardo in the battle that he hoped to evade by leaving in the first place. Together, they embark on a gripping adventure that will test not just their ethics, but their convictions and resolve.

ISBN: 9789609278508

About the Author

A lifelong learner and impassioned seeker of human potential, Alex Alvarez has journeyed through a multicultural life, guided by the power of strong bonds across borders. Yet, he found his most fulfilling experience in becoming a father. Faced with a cancer diagnosis, he made the poignant decision to craft a lasting legacy for his young daughter—a book brimming with life lessons, paternal insights, and overall, unconditional love.

A spirited individual radiating an unquenchable zest for life, Alex is a steadfast believer in the transformative power of resilience, gratitude, and familial connections. His seminal work, *Dad's Wisdom: A Blueprint for Life*, is more than just a book; it's a compendium of actionable advice and heartfelt storytelling aimed not only at providing inspiration for his daughter but also at sparking a generational shift towards purposeful and meaningful living.

***

Don't be shy. Say hello!
aaalvarezpublishing@outlook.com

www.ingramcontent.com/pod-product-compliance
Lightning Source LLC
Chambersburg PA
CBHW020749230426
43665CB00009B/544